Gangsters and
G-Men on Screen

Gangsters and G-Men on Screen

Crime Cinema Then and Now

Gene D. Phillips

Rowman & Littlefield
Lanham • Boulder • New York • Toronto • Plymouth, UK

Published by Rowman & Littlefield
4501 Forbes Boulevard, Suite 200, Lanham, Maryland 20706
www.rowman.com

10 Thornbury Road, Plymouth PL6 7PP, United Kingdom

British Library Cataloguing in Publication Information Available

Library of Congress Cataloging-in-Publication Data

Phillips, Gene D.
  Gangsters and G-men on screen : crime cinema then and now / Gene D. Phillips.
    pages cm
  Includes bibliographical references and index.
  ISBN 978-1-4422-3075-0 (hardback : alk. paper) — ISBN 978-1-4422-3076-7
(ebook) 1. Gangster films—History and criticism. I. Title.
  PN1995.9.G3P45 2014
  791.43'6556—dc23   2014012122

For James M. Welsh

CONTENTS

CONTENTS

ACKNOWLEDGMENTS

I am especially grateful to the filmmakers who discussed their films with me during the long period in which I was developing this project. I interviewed John Huston, Arthur Penn, and Martin Scorsese in New York, and Fritz Lang and William Wyler in Hollywood. I also talked with Francis Ford Coppola at the Cannes International Film Festival.

I would also like to mention the staffs of the Film Study Center of the Museum of Modern Art in New York; the Margaret Herrick Library of the Academy of Motion Picture Arts and Sciences in Beverly Hills, California; the Motion Picture Section of the Library of Congress in Washington, D.C.; and the Special Collections of the Newberry Library in Chicago.

Some material in this book previously appeared in a completely different form in the following publications: "Faulkner and the Film," *Literature/Film Quarterly* 1, no. 3 (Summer 1973): 263–73, copyright 1973, by Salisbury University; "Fritz Lang Remembers," *Focus on Film* (London) 5, no. 2 (Spring 1975): 43–51; "William Wyler," *Focus on Film* (London) 5, no. 2 (Spring 1976): 5–10; *Major Film Directors of the American and British Cinema* (Cranbury, N.J.: Associated University Presses, 1999), copyright 1999, by Associated University Presses; *Godfather: The Intimate Francis Ford Coppola* (Lexington: University of Kentucky Press, 2004), copyright 2004, by University of Kentucky Press.

INTRODUCTION
In Search of the Gangster Genre

The gangster film has been part of the Hollywood output for a century; indeed, its "persistent popularity is unequaled in Hollywood history."[1] Yet, the gangster film has been slighted by a number of critics and film historians alike, not because it is artistically inferior to other types of film, but because it deals with the "tawdry and unpleasant aspects of American life."[2] In short, it focuses on the kind of violent conflicts that other movies tend to gloss over.

If one peruses the motion picture section of a university library, one will notice that there are far more books devoted to other genres, for instance, the western, than the gangster film. Consequently, this book highlights a variety of significant gangster movies, for example, such classic gangster movies as *Little Caesar* and *The Public Enemy*. But it also features movies like *The Lady from Shanghai*, a well-known thriller that is not considered a gangster film. As Colin McArthur opines in *Underworld USA*, one of the first important books on the gangster film, there is no reason why a picture like *The Lady from Shanghai* cannot be related by "iconography and personnel" to more than one type of film.[3] Moreover, this study includes neglected gangster pictures the likes of *The Story of Temple Drake*, derived from William Faulkner's notorious novel *Sanctuary*, as an indication that there are more gangster films of worth than one might assume.

In sum, this book presents an in-depth discussion of several gangster films, some of which are familiar members of the gangster genre, like John

Huston's *The Asphalt Jungle*, and some that deserve to be better known, for example, Stephen Frears's *The Grifters*.

That a few meaningful books on the gangster film have appeared throughout the years demonstrates the continued interest in the genre. These include Carlos Clarens's *Crime Movies: An Illustrated History of the Gangster Genre from D. W. Griffith to* Pulp Fiction (1980), with an afterword by Foster Hirsch that updates the book (1997); Marilyn Yaquinto's *Pump 'Em Full of Lead: A Look at Gangsters on Film* (1998); Jack Shadoian's *Dreams and Dead Ends: The American Gangster Film*, 2nd ed. (2003), first printed in 1977; and Thomas Leitch's *Crime Films* (2002), reprinted in 2009.

McArthur's *Underworld USA* (1972) is a groundbreaking book on the gangster genre, but it covers only a few major crime films. By the same token, Douglas Brode's *Money, Women, and Guns: Crime Movies from* Bonnie and Clyde *to the Present* (1995) presents commentary on a selection of mostly standard gangster pictures, whereas in this volume, I include some overlooked crime movies that deserve more attention than they have received. In addition, I have interviewed film directors, as well as other artists and technicians, associated with the films I treat. I also focus on some more recent movies, along with some from the classic period. These later movies are reminders that the gangster genre is still with us and is not going away.

THE RISE OF THE GANGSTER FILM

The city has always been looked upon as the Citadel of Sin in gangster movies because of the huge influx of immigrants to this country. Between 1880 and 1914, the overcrowded slums of such cities as New York and Chicago were seedbeds of criminality. In brief, the rise of gangsters was the result of the "corruption and impersonality" of the modern city.[1]

The immigrant population observed that only the gangs defied the corrupt cops and city officials, and so the gangs found their recruits in the mean streets of big U.S. cities. During the era of silent pictures (in round numbers, 1895–1928), films often reflected the plight of the immigrants.[2] "We were always conscious," writes Robert Warshow in his celebrated essay "The Gangster as Tragic Hero," that the whole meaning of the gangster's career is in a "drive for success; the typical gangster film presents a steady upward progress, followed by a very precipitate fall."[3]

The gangster movie actually put its happy ending in the middle, when the criminal is enjoying the fruits of his ill-gotten gains. The end of the picture depicts his tragic downfall, as he grimly meets his fate.

The gangster genre was born in the silent era, with pioneer director D. W. Griffith's two-reeler, *The Muskateers of Pig Alley*. In 1912, Griffith made this eighteen-minute movie (muskateer was another name for hoodlum in those days[4]), which is generally considered the first real gangster picture. The Biograph Film Company, where Griffith worked, was located on New York's seedy Lower East Side. Griffith filmed the exterior scenes in the backstreets and alleys of the neighborhood.

Griffith tore the movie's plot from the headlines of the day. At two reels, the film was the standard length of movies of that time. In fact, Griffith shot 485 Biograph shorts between 1908 and 1915, before moving on to features. Some of them, like *The Muskateers of Pig Alley*, were mini-masterpieces.

The Muskateers of Pig Alley (1912)

The heroine, called the "Little Lady" (Lillian Gish), is picked up by a gangster who happens to be the leader of a local gang. He escorts her to a dance hall, where he buys her a drink. He surreptitiously drops a Mickey Finn in her glass, with a view to seducing her, but the Snapper Kid (Elmer Booth), the leader of a rival mob, sees what the other gangster is up to and swiftly interferes by sending the Little Lady home. His action angers the other mob boss, who had designs on the Little Lady, and he instigates a gun battle between the two rival mobs in Pig Alley, which is close to the dance hall.

On their way to the gun battle, Snapper and his sidekick (Harry Carey) sneak down the alley, creeping toward the camera along a brick wall, until the Snapper's menacing face fills the screen in a breathtaking close-up. The shootout erupts, and the bodies of dead gangsters litter the alley. When it is over, a cop, with a wink, directs Snapper toward a saloon door. It opens just enough for a hand to reach out and offer him a wad of bills. The printed title on the screen reads, "Links in a chain." Here, Griffith ironically suggests that gangsters like Snapper regularly accept bribes from the police. Griffith's point is about graft in the police force (Snapper has apparently done a favor for the cops and is in their pay).

The director implies that the city is a decadent society, where the police are in cahoots with criminals like the Snapper. Furthermore, the gangsters' world, as adroitly pictured by Griffith, is replete with "bars, alleys, dance halls, guns, cops, loyal sidekicks, and rival gangs."[5] All in all, *The Muskateers of Pig Alley* is an excellent little movie, with Elmer Clifton, an experienced stage actor, stealing the show as a skilled thief. Harry Carey went on to star in several silent westerns directed by John Ford.

Marilyn Yaquinto notes that Raoul Walsh's relatively unknown *Regeneration* (1915) is often thought of as a fine early example of the gangster genre.[6] Admittedly, at seventy-two minutes, it is feature-length, whereas

Griffith's Biograph short is not. But Walsh's movie was not as influential as *The Muskateers of Pig Alley* precisely because it was not as widely seen as Griffith's film. *Regeneration* is the work of a talented but inexperienced amateur. What's more, Walsh's sinister tenement corridors and grubby street scenes recall Griffith's camera work in his gangster film and attest to Griffith's influence on Walsh, who had been Griffith's assistant.

Movies did not begin evolving a grimmer atmosphere and darker vision until after World War I. In Berlin, Fritz Lang's work was developing toward his 1922 breakthrough film, a gangster picture entitled *Dr. Mabuse, der Spieler* (*Dr. Mabuse, the Gambler*). Lang directed this, his first gangster film, depicting Germany's demoralized state after the nation's defeat in World War I. It was the sort of atmosphere in which an arch criminal like Mabuse could thrive, for crime was rampant in postwar Germany.

Mabuse is particularly adept at hypnotizing people to get them to further his nefarious schemes. As a master of disguise, he eludes capture. The movie's climax is a gun battle between Mabuse's mob and the police, as the cops lay siege to Mabuse's hideout. This final gun battle is

Fritz Lang made an early gangster picture in Germany in 1922, *Dr. Mabuse, der Spieler* (*Dr. Mabuse, the Gambler*), a silent film.

3

photographed in a spare, newsreel-like style that recalls the final shoot-out in *The Musketeers of Pig Alley*. The street outside Mabuse's hangout fills with smoke from gunfire and exploding grenades.

Lang's successful film helped popularize gangster movies in Europe. When Lang migrated to Hollywood in the wake of the rise of Hitler in 1933, the director's full mastery of the gangster genre was evident in his American films (see chapter 6).

Underworld (1927)

Josef von Sternberg, who, like Lang, was born in Austria, immigrated to the United States as a teenager and finally settled in Hollywood to learn the craft of motion pictures in 1924. In 1927, he directed *Underworld*, widely regarded as the "prototype of the modern gangster film."[7] Von Sternberg made the movie during Prohibition (which ran from 1920 to the early 1930s). It was a time when "drinkers paid more for worse booze. Fishermen became rum runners. Politicians became gangsters. Gangsters became legends."[8] The public broke the law by imbibing bootleg whiskey in illegal speakeasies. Indeed, *Underworld* portrays criminals as appealing characters helping ordinary people get the alcohol the government had outlawed.

Paramount commissioned former Chicago journalist Ben Hecht to write a prose treatment (detailed plot summary) for a film about organized crime, apparently set in Chicago, although the city is never named in the picture. In a brief essay that is part of his private papers, Hecht recalls his days as a reporter in Chicago, writing, "I got out after sixteen years of chasing fires, killers, swindles, and scandals."[9] The studio turned over Hecht's eighteen-page scenario to screenwriter Robert N. Lee, and the resulting script was given to von Sternberg to direct.

Hecht later complained that von Sternberg "ruined" the shooting script with his changes. Actually, von Sternberg jettisoned some minor characters and simplified the story line—all of which improved the screenplay. The central character, gangster "Bull" Weed (George Bancroft), became a sensitive, sensible man, whereas Hecht saw him as a primitive lout who would not win audience sympathy the way that von Sternberg's Bull Weed would. Hecht disowned the finished film—until he received an Oscar at the very first Academy Award ceremonies for his original story.

Bull Weed, as von Sternberg envisions him, is an underworld kingpin; he is also a self-made man who hires a disbarred lawyer called "Rolls Royce" as his mouthpiece. Bull smiles when he notices an investment company's advertisement, proclaiming, "The city is yours!" His smile signifies his determination to be a success. At the end of the picture, Bull allows his gun moll, "Feather" (Evelyn Brent), and Rolls Royce, who have fallen in love, to escape from a police raid on his hideout, instead of seeking revenge for their deceit. That leaves Bull to face the cops alone as they invade his stronghold. He thus sacrifices himself for his lover and best friend.

Hence, the moviegoing public found Bull a fundamentally sympathetic character, and *Underworld* "connected with a wide audience." The picture launched the gangster movie as a popular genre.[10] In addition, Evelyn Brent's cool, sensual performance as Feathers prefigured the parts that Marlene Dietrich would play for von Sternberg in films like *Shanghai Express* (1932).

Underworld was enhanced by von Sternberg's superb visual imagery, with its moon-flooded, forbidding streets starkly lit by ace cinematographer

Evelyn Brent as the gun moll "Feathers" in Josef von Sternberg's *Underworld* (1927), the first iconic ganster film. Howard Hawks named the heroine of *Rio Bravo* (1959) "Feathers" as an homage to von Sternberg.

Bert Glennon. And the principal setting, a basement speakeasy called the Dreamland Café, is a "close, windowless environment" that typifies the underworld where the principal characters live out their lives.[11]

The gangster genre got a transfusion of new life with the advent of sound pictures in late 1927, when Alan Crosland's *The Jazz Singer* premiered on October 6 and inaugurated the era of sound pictures in Hollywood. The film, starring Al Jolson, features a musical score and four musical numbers—but only one dialogue sequence. It was followed in July 1928, by Bryan Foy's *The Lights of New York*, a gangster movie that was the first all-talking picture.

Ernest Hemingway's terse, crisp dialogue in his 1927 short story "The Killers" became the model for the hard-bitten, brittle dialogue in gangster pictures during the sound period. When a racketeer in *The Lights of New York* orders a mob hit, he says, "Take him for a ride," thereby sealing the victim's doom. The phrase is still used in contemporary gangster movies. It signifies that the victim is "taking a ride" from which he will not return.

In her book *American Gangster Cinema*, Fran Mason writes perceptively that the advent of sound pictures was an important development for the gangster genre. The gangsters' slang and the "gunshots and screeching tires, as well as background noises of the city environment, more fully evoked the . . . world that the gangster inhabited."[12]

The plot of *The Lights of New York* concerns two country bumpkins who come to New York to open a barber shop, which soon becomes a front for a gang of bootleggers. The theme of the innocent country boys being corrupted by city slickers resonated in other gangster films of the time. Bryan Foy once told me that the movie was a hit because of the "novelty of sound"—otherwise it is a routine gangster picture. The coming of sound took Hollywood by storm, Foy continued, "as the studios frantically rushed to convert to sound." By 1929, the "sound era was in full swing," he concluded,[13] and, by 1930, gangster movies were gaining in popularity, with the help of some gangster movies that remain classics today.

CHAPTER TWO
LITTLE CAESAR AND THE PUBLIC ENEMY

The antiheroes of the gangster pictures of the 1930s were primarily based on real-life criminals from the preceding decade. When Prohibition was in force, such gangster movies as *Little Caesar*, *The Public Enemy*, and *Scarface* gave us a vision of the underside of American life represented by tawdry poolrooms, stale cigarette smoke, naked lightbulbs, and dark alleys. Depression audiences were gratified to see criminals in gangster movies stealing from the wealthy in their ruthless rise to the top.

Warner Bros. conceived *Little Caesar* (1930) to be a thinly disguised portrait of Al Capone. Despite the fact that Edward G. Robinson, who played the Capone character, was born in Bucharest, Romania, he did look something like the Italian Capone. The director, Mervyn LeRoy, was not yet an experienced filmmaker, but he wisely had Robinson smoking a cigar, since Capone was often seen with one. Sensing that the movie would attract a large audience, Warner rushed *The Public Enemy* into production for release in 1931. Similarly, producer Howard Hughes prepared *Scarface* for filming posthaste, but Hughes ran into censorship problems regarding the liberal helpings of sex and violence in the movie; he bickered with the Hays Office, supervised by the censorship chief, Will Hays, for some time, so that *Scarface* was delayed for more than year. It was not released until 1932.

Capone got to hear about *Little Caesar* and *Scarface* being based on him (Capone's nickname was "Scarface"). He sent two of his henchmen to see Ben Hecht, who was writing the screenplay for *Scarface*, to inquire about how their boss would be portrayed on the screen. Hecht reassured the two gangsters that Hollywood was not turning out a film about Capone, but the studios wanted the public to think that they were because that would attract the mass audience to see it. "That's part of the racket that we call showmanship," Hecht explained.[1] The two hoodlums bought his explanation.

Little Caesar (1930)

There is no doubt that novelist and screenwriter W. R. (William Reilly) Burnett wrote the novel on which the film *Little Caesar* is based and devised some episodes in the book as analogues to Capone' s life. Burnett was born in Springfield, Ohio (as was the author of this book). Having grown up in a small Midwestern town, he moved to Chicago in the mid-1920s, a more suitable setting for the crime fiction he wanted to write. There Burnett encountered the sort of tough gangsters he had never met in Ohio. He created Caesar Enrico Bandello for his 1929 novel *Little Caesar* as an anti-Horatio Alger character, one who would be destroyed by his own vaunting ambition.

Burnett wrote the novel from the point of view of Rico, alias Little Caesar. Thus, the novelist presents the underworld as "seen completely through the eyes of a gangster,"[2] with the story told by Rico in his own mean street vernacular. The book's gangsters, which the average reader had never previously encountered before, delighted the public, and Warner Bros. snapped up the screen rights.

Jack Warner, the production chief, assigned Mervyn LeRoy, a young contract director, to *Little Caesar*. LeRoy had made such lightweight films as *Harold Teen* (1928), but he would make his mark in Hollywood with stark crime dramas like *Little Caesar*. Screenwriters Robert Lee (*Underworld*) and Francis Faragoh were at pains to give depth to the characters in the script. For example, the relationship of Rico and his young sidekick, Joe Masara (Douglas Fairbanks Jr.), is more developed in the film than in the book. Joe wants to escape the underworld in favor of earning an honest living as a dancer, while Rico sees Joe's aspirations to leave him as a betrayal of their friendship.

8

The colloquial dialogue, jazzy musical score (reminiscent of the Jazz Age), and realistic sound effects serve to effectively delineate the gangster genre. Prohibition drew to a close in early 1933, and "as it did so, the gang wars escalated."[3] The St. Valentine's Day Massacre, by which Al Capone had seven members of Bugsy Segal's rival gang eliminated in a Clark Street garage in Chicago, focused public attention on organized crime. The mob wars in Chicago were very much a part of the plot of *Little Caesar*, which tracks the rise and fall of Rico, a small-time hood, and his efforts to rule the rackets in Chicago.

Rico therefore exemplifies Robert Warshow's description of the gangster as a tragic hero because his arrogant obsession with becoming a crime lord leads to his downfall. For criminals like Rico, the American Dream degenerates into a nightmare. He wanted desperately to be a somebody, and instead he winds up in skid row as a nobody.

Shooting the picture went smoothly. The cinematographer was Tony Gaudio, who began his career at the time *The Musketeers of Pig Alley* was made. He chose to photograph the present film in harsh lighting, which was appropriate for the gritty gangster setting. The critics noted that the fact that the picture portrayed three-dimensional characters made the movie all the more interesting and chilling.

LeRoy demonstrated his mastery of the film medium at this early stage in his movie career by his judicious employment of close-ups. "There aren't many," Jack Shadoian points out, "but when they come, their impact justifies LeRoy's choices and selectivity."[4] For example, when Joe informs Rico that he has decided to drop out of the gang, a close-up of Rico portrays his disappointment and bewilderment.

When *Little Caesar* was submitted to the Hays Office, Will Hays and his board of consulters were concerned that the upwardly mobile Rico would appear to be an attractive character to members of the mass audience, especially ambitious youngsters. Jason Joy, Hays's chief consulter, defended the movie against such complaints from church groups who had previewed the picture, contending that the film taught a stern moral lesson that crime does not pay.[5]

Back in the day, certain states maintained their own censorship boards, among them New York. The New York Board demanded several censorial cuts before it would allow the picture to be exhibited there. Warner

Bros. made a token emendation to the film before its release. When the police gun down Rico in the street, he mutters, "Mother of Mercy, is this the end of Rico?" The line originally went, "Mother of God, is this the end of Rico?" The studio assumed that this minor alteration would mollify the religious right, who were protesting the picture, but to no avail.

In the end, comments Gregory Black, *Little Caesar* played without cuts throughout the country (although not in New York), "without releasing new crime waves in the rest of the nation."[6] When the picture opened in early 1931, crowds mobbed the box office to see it, and it continued to do big business nationwide.

Little Caesar begins with a shot of the front cover of Burnett's novel, followed by a quotation from the New Testament of the Bible: "For all those who take the sword will perish with the sword" (Matthew 26:52). This Bible passage was yet another attempt on the part of Warner Bros. to convince the religious organizations who protested the film that it did, in fact, have a moral message.

The film proper opens with a long shot of a sinister figure getting out of a car and entering an isolated gas station late at night. The lights go out in the station, and two gun shots pierce the darkness. The man emerges from the gas station and gets into the car, and the driver takes off. Rico, the gunman, and Joe, the driver, then stop at an all-night diner for spaghetti. Rico tells Joe he is tired of being a penny-ante crook; he and Joe are accordingly moving on to the big city (Chicago), where they can become big-time operators.

In the big town, Joe hooks up with Olga (Glenda Farrell) as her dancing partner in a nightclub act. Rico observes sarcastically, "Dancin' just ain't my idea of a man's game." He joins a mob bossed by Sam Vettori (Stanley Fields) and then plans a daring New Year's Eve heist at the Brass Peacock Club, where Joe and Olga perform. Rico forces Joe to participate in the robbery. During the course of the robbery, Rico shoots Crime Commissioner McClure for good measure. A Hollywood wag once described *Little Caesar* as a series of catastrophes leading up to a floor show. The movie does fit this description when one contemplates the New Year's Eve sequence.

Rico inevitably takes over as chief of Vettori's gang, telling Sam, "You just sit around cheating yourself at solitaire. You've got so that you can dish it out, but you can't take it no more. You're through!" He warns the gang members, "If anyone turns yellow and squeals, my gun is going to speak its piece." For an early sound movie, *Little Caesar* has some memorable bits of dialogue.

Rico makes good on his threat to the mob when he hears that Tony Passa, one of the gang members, is going to confess his crimes to the parish priest of his boyhood, Father McNeil. He catches up with Tony and guns him down ruthlessly on the steps of the church. Rico has made a number of enemies on his way to the top, and a rival gang leader arranges a drive-by shooting to exterminate him. When Rico is shot at from a milk truck, he is stunned by a bullet that just misses wounding him critically. He has been jolted into realizing that, even though he is a mob kingpin, he is, after all, a vulnerable human being.

Rico has a subconscious homosexual attachment to Joe that he does not fully understand. He does, however, suspect that he "likes Joe too much." When Joe finally insists that he is going to leave the rackets for good, Rico is devastated that Joe is no longer willing to be subservient to him.[7] Rico threatens to shoot Joe on the spot but cannot bring himself to do it. When Joe walks out on him, Rico has no real allies left, so he must go into hiding. He reflects, "This is what I get for liking a guy too much."

After Joe's "betrayal" of him, Rico hides out for a time in the cellar of Ma Magdalena's produce store. Les and Barbara Keyser describe Ma as the "wicked witch of the decade."[8] She is played by Lucille La Verne, who capped her career in pictures by voicing the wicked witch in *Snow White and the Seven Dwarfs* (1937).

The members of Rico's mob gradually abandon him, and a printed statement on the screen states, "Months passed. Rico's course had been like a skyrocket—starting in the gutter and returning there." Sergeant Tom Flaherty (Thomas Jackson), the cop who had been pursuing Rico throughout the movie, plants an item in the local newspaper calling Rico a yellow coward for going into hiding. Rico is outraged when he reads the article while staying in the flophouse, where he has reached the nadir of his downward spiral. He phones Flaherty and savagely threatens to get even with him for smearing his name. Flaherty has the call traced and soon tracks Rico down in a deserted backstreet. LeRoy photographs Rico in long shot, emphasizing his insignificance. Flaherty fires a submachine gun into the billboard behind which Rico is hiding. Rico dies, murmuring, "Mother of Mercy, is this the end of Rico?"

Edward G. Robinson in the title role of Little Caesar (1930), directed by Mervyn LeRoy.

The poster for the talking picture on the billboard that Rico was taking cover behind is for a musical entitled *Tipsy Topsy Turvy*, starring none other than Joe and Olga, Joe's dancing partner. The musical's title is a metaphor for Rico's unstable existence. The Hays Office passed *Little Caesar* for exhibition without any cuts because Rico's career trajectory, which led to his degradation, warned moviegoers that criminals come to an ignominious end when the party is over.

Little Caesar is a milestone in the history of the gangster genre. According to Kathryn Osenlund, "It consolidated all the essential scenes of the American gangster's rise and fall"—his joining a big city mob and eventually taking it over, and "his final, pathetic fall from power and grace."[9]

Gratified by the huge success of *Little Caesar*, Warner Bros. rushed another gangster picture into theaters a scant three months after the release of LeRoy's gangster film. Warner specialized in movies about gangsters and films that deal with social problems. They wanted *The Public Enemy* to be both.

The Public Enemy (1931)

The Public Enemy portrays how the sordid slums in which youngsters grow up in a big city contribute to the "evolution of the criminal."[10] Accordingly, producers decided to begin this film with the following printed prologue: "It is the ambition of the authors of *The Public Enemy* to depict honestly the environment that exists today in certain strata of American life, rather than to glorify the hoodlum or the criminal."

Darryl Zanuck, who was production chief at Warner Bros. (under the supervision of Jack Warner) at the time, opted to have William Wellman replace Archie Mayo as director of *The Public Enemy* (Mayo would later direct Humphrey Bogart in a major gangster movie, *The Petrified Forest*). Wellman had made *Wings* (1927), the first film ever to win the Academy Award for Best Picture.

When production commenced on *The Public Enemy*, Edward Woods was to play the lead, an Irish gangster named Tom Powers, while James Cagney was slated to play Tom's buddy, Matt Doyle. After Wellman had viewed the first three days of rushes, he contacted Zanuck and said, "Look, there is a horrible mistake—we have the wrong guy—Cagney should be the lead."[11] In *Beer and Blood: Enemies of the Public*, the documentary that accompanies the DVD of *The Public Enemy*, Martin Scorsese (*The Departed*) mentions that Cagney had just finished a picture called *The Millionaire*, in which he demonstrated that he knew the "New York lingo." Cagney was a red-haired Irishman, the product of New York's Lower East Side (where Griffith had shot the exteriors for *The Musketeers of Pig Alley*). The actor could play a tough customer with a gruff voice like Tom Powers. "Wellman's nickname was 'Wild Bill,'" Scorsese continues, "because he was ferocious when he was making a film he believed in."[12]

Wellman was a hard-working, hard-drinking director who quarreled with producers, as well as with actors. He was of Anglo-Irish descent and a juvenile delinquent in his youth. Thus, he knew the world of Tom Powers. "His best work was stamped with a characteristic vigor and toughness that ranks him with action directors like Raoul Walsh (*White Heat*)."[13] Wellman went on to make *Wild Boys of the Road* (1937), a social protest film about rough youngsters during the Depression who had to cheat and steal, not to get ahead, but just to survive.

Kubec Glasmon, a Chicago druggist, and John Bright, a former reporter for the *Chicago Evening Post*, published a novel entitled *Beer and Blood*. It came to Zanuck's attention, and he bought the screen rights. The coauthors of the book subsequently received an Oscar nomination for Best Original Story. Warner Bros. commissioned Harvey Thew to turn the book into a screenplay entitled *The Public Enemy*. The novel is based on the exploits of Dion "Deanie" O'Bannion, chief of the Irish Mafia in Chicago, and two bootleggers, Frankie Lake and Terry Duggan. Wellman shot the film "on the double" (in a speedy twenty-six days) and "on the cheap" (at a stringent cost of $151,000).[14]

There is a scene near the end of the shooting script that was not filmed. When Tom's brother Mike, a veteran of World War I, discovers Tom's death in a gangland shooting, he stuffs hand grenades like those he used during the war in France in his overcoat pockets. The script states that Mike goes off to avenge Tom's murder, suggesting that his brother's fate has "turned Mike into a killer."[15] The studio decided that having a war hero portrayed as a murderer was an affront to the veterans of the war and scuttled the scene.

Nevertheless, Warner Bros. did not escape other objections leveled at the film. As it happened, the Hays Office promulgated to the film industry its Motion Picture Production Code on March 31, 1930, but the studios largely ignored it, thereby drawing fire from religious and parent groups (the code would not be fully implemented until 1934). The code declares that a movie "appeals to every class, mature and immature," and it also states concern for the manner in which sex and violence, in particular, affect young and impressionable moviegoers.[16]

Yet, concerned citizens complained to the Hays Office that the spate of gangster pictures inaugurated by *Little Caesar* and carried on by such movies as *The Public Enemy* were filled with trigger-happy racketeers, wisecracking gun molls, and lawless gangs. As Carlos Clarens puts it in his thought-provoking book *Crime Movies*, "For a good part of *The Public Enemy* the message appeared to be, it's a helluva lot of fun to bootleg and shoot it out with rival gangs."[17]

On the credit side of the ledger, however, it must be noted that much of the violence in *The Public Enemy* takes place offscreen, as when Tom takes revenge on Putty Nose, the gangster whom he believes let him and his buddy Matt down. Putty Nose pleads for his life while playing the piano for Tom and Matt, just like he once did when they were teenagers. Wellman's camera focuses on Matt while Tom brutally murders Putty Nose. Matt is sickened by watching Tom as shots ring out and Putty Nose's body slumps onto the keyboard with a crash of discordant piano keys. Showing Matt's reaction to the slaying is an excellent use of artistic indirection, for it implies the gruesome deed without showing it on the screen.

Will Hays and his confederates cut the movie from ninety-six to eighty-four minutes in an attempt to keep the film from endorsing the life of a tough mobster. Nevertheless, the distinguished critic-at-large Lincoln Kirstein, in his essay "James Cagney and the American Hero," maintains that Tom is presented as an American hero in the movie. According to Kirstein, Cagney plays Tom as a criminal who is "quick to wrath" and "articulate in anger. No one expresses more clearly in terms of pictorial action the delights of violence, the overtones of semiconscious sadism," and the tendency toward anarchy than Cagney as Tom Powers.[18]

Doubt was openly expressed in the press about Warner Bros.' contention that this film was made to depict how youngsters growing up in a sordid environment are influenced by corrupt adults to become gangsters. One critic, representing the National Board of Review, countered the studio's stance by contending that to say that gangsters are bred in the slums is "pretty superficial and unconvincing: Tom Powers seemed to be a bad lot from the beginning."[19]

The Public Enemy starts out with a printed prologue (quoted earlier), which more than one reviewer dismissed as Warner Bros.' sociological alibi for making the picture. The opening credits are accompanied by the old favorite song, "I'm Forever Blowing Bubbles," but it is played in a sinister, minor key, as befits a gangster picture. The movie is bookended by the song, which is played in the final scene on a phonograph, in a sentimental rendition.

The film proper begins in 1909, with Tom (Frank Coghlan) as a mischievous street urchin, complete with cap and knickers, living in a lower-class Irish neighborhood. His father is a brutish policeman who treats Tom harshly because he fears Tom is becoming a ruffian. By contrast, his doting mother is simply unaware that her son is turning into a juvenile delinquent. Tom mocks his straight-arrow brother Mike for going to school "to learn how to be poor." Tom regularly plays hooky with his pal Mike Doyle (Frankie Darro, who would play the lead in Wellman's *Wild Boys of the Road*).

By 1915, Tom (Cagney) has grown into a petty hoodlum, still hanging around with Matt (Edward Woods). Tom and Matt join a gang of ruffians run by Putty Nose, a racketeer who gives them their first guns to use in an armed robbery. When Prohibition comes in 1920, Tom and Matt are invited by Paddy Ryan (Robert Emmett O'Connor) to join his mob of bootleggers. They begin to make easy money, delivering illegal alcohol in a phony gasoline truck to saloons.

Tom's big brother Mike (Donald Cook) comes home from the army suffering from shell shock (called battle fatigue by the army). Ma Powers (Beryl Mercer) has a dinner to welcome Mike home. Tom and Matt show up with a keg of beer, which they dump in the middle of the dining room table. Mike flies into a rage, exclaiming, "You murderers! There is not only beer in that keg! There is beer and blood!" Mike shatters the keg against the wall. Tom sneers at his brother and stalks out of the house, thereby severing ties with his family. This is the scene in the book from which Burnett drew the title of the novel.

Tom moves in with his girlfriend Kitty (Mae Clarke). One morning he has a hangover and snaps at Kitty that he is tired of her nagging. He grabs half a grapefruit from the breakfast table and mashes it in Kitty's face. Cagney was supposed to threaten Kitty with the grapefruit, not push it in her face, comments Drew Casper, and so Clarke's shocked reaction was genuine.[20]

Shortly afterward, Tom has a fling with Gwen Allen (played by Jean Harlow, who became an icon of 1930s Hollywood cinema; Harlow had a Bronx accent, so, like Cagney, she knew the New York lingo). At one point, Gwen lays Tom's head on her breast and murmurs, "You're a spoiled boy, Tommy." She is more right than she realizes, for Tom is an immature boy who has never really grown up (his mother also calls him Tommy). But Tom resents her suggesting that he is a "mamma's boy," and that is the end of their relationship.

Paddy Ryan warns his mob that trouble is brewing with Schemer Burns's gang, which is on the prowl. Soon thereafter Matt Doyle is mowed down with a submachine gun in a daring daylight shooting on the street. Tom vows vengeance on the Burns gang for murdering his boyhood friend. Tom goes straight to Burns's headquarters in a down-

James Cagney (center) as Tom Powers in *The Public Enemy* (1931), which made Cagney a star. Cagney is flanked by Edward Woods as his accomplice and Beryl Mercer as his mother.

pour; the camera remains outside while Tom marches into Burns's lair. We hear—but do not see—a savage shootout. Tom, all blood spattered, stumbles out onto the street; he mutters, "I ain't so tough," and falls forward into the gutter. Like Rico before him, Tom is forced to admit that he is not invincible, but rather a vulnerable human being. Once again the gory violence takes place offscreen.

Tom's mother and brother come to see him in the hospital, where he is swathed in bandages. It is a family reunion for Ma Powers and her two sons (her husband is long since dead). Ma still blindly believes that Tom is a "good boy who got in with the wrong crowd," as she says. Tom wants to return to his mother's hearth and home to recuperate.

Ma Powers is preparing a family dinner for Tom's homecoming. Mike answers the phone and is told that Tom is on his way home. The Victrola in the living room is playing "I'm Forever Blowing Bubbles." Mike answers the doorbell, only to be confronted with Tom's corpse, still wrapped in hospital bandages and riddled with bullets, standing erect for a moment in the doorway. Then the corpse falls forward toward the camera and lands facedown on the floor.

Mike, who is devastated by the ghastly sight of his brother's corpse, walks directly toward the camera as he goes to his mother to reveal the gruesome news of Tom's homecoming and thus burst her bubble about the happy homecoming of her beloved son. The film's final shot shows the phonograph needle churning endlessly at the end of the record. The song, which implies the futility of Tom's ambitions, is over. Kirstein observes that the final scene leaves the impression about Tom that there was "something likeable and courageous about the little rat after all."[21] This is precisely what troubled some reviewers: They feared that many moviegoers found Tom Powers a sympathetic character. Since the Hays Office had already snipped twelve minutes out of the film, they were not inclined to cut the film further before its release, but as the movie played throughout the country, the guardians of morality complained vociferously that Hollywood had to stop making lawbreakers look so appealing. "Tragic" gangsters should not be tolerated on the screen.[22]

In defending the picture, Warner Bros. pointed to the printed epilogue at film's end: "The end of Tom Powers is the end of every hoodlum. The public enemy is not a man or a character. It is a problem that we must solve." Interestingly enough, when *Little Caesar* and *The Public Enemy* were rereleased on a double bill in 1954, as the toughest of the gangster films, the foreword to the double bill virtually repeated the epilogue of *The Public Enemy*.

Withal, at the time of the original release of *The Public Enemy*, there were those who saw it as a film of quality. *Variety* lauded the movie as the "roughest, most powerful, and best gangster film to date."[23] Moreover, Wellman's reputation as a major film director is founded on films like *The Public Enemy*, which stands above most other gangster films of the era. It boasts the top-flight performances of Cagney and Harlow, as well as vivid action scenes that remain potent today.

CHAPTER THREE

THE STORY OF TEMPLE DRAKE AND NO ORCHIDS FOR MISS BLANDISH

The Story of Temple Drake (1933)

The last significant gangster film to appear before the Hays Office enforced the Motion Picture Production Code was *The Story of Temple Drake* (1933).[1] The movie was derived from a controversial novel by William Faulkner entitled *Sanctuary* (1931). The novel caused a scandal, and Faulkner later admitted that it was written in part to turn a profit. He was growing weary of writing novels "that got published but not bought," he confides in his introduction to the 1932 Modern Library edition. So he "invented the most horrific tale" he could imagine to create a certain best seller.[2]

Although *Sanctuary* is a deeply serious work of art, there are, to be sure, some "horrific" elements in the novel, founded on conversations Faulkner had during his occasional tours of some Memphis nightspots. He met one young woman, who told him about a bootlegger named Neal "Popeye" Pumphrey, a gangster thought to be impotent.[3] Because the film departs from the novel in many ways, it is necessary to outline the book before considering the movie's literary source.

In the novel, Temple Drake is a frivolous, flirtatious female college student. She goes on a date with her beau, Gowan Stevens. He gets drunk and takes her to the Old Frenchman's Place, a haven for bootleggers, to get more liquor. There Gowan and his girl encounter a group of lowlifes: Lee Goodwin and Ruby, his common-law wife; Popeye, a Memphis gangster, and some fellow racketeers; and Tommy, a mentally retarded handyman. Gowan eventually sobers up and sneaks back to town, leaving Temple stranded with the bootleggers. Ruby assigns Tommy to guard Temple, but Popeye shoots Tommy dead and rapes Temple with a corn cob, since he is impotent.

Popeye takes Temple to Miss Reba's bordello in Memphis, where he provides her with a companion, a gangster named Alabama Red, so he can watch them together. Temple stays on at the brothel for a while because she is fascinated by Popeye's perverse world. Meanwhile, Lee is accused of Tommy's murder, and his lawyer, Horace Benbow, tracks down Temple at Miss Reba's. But Temple refuses to testify on Lee's behalf, lest all the scandalous facts of the case would be revealed in open court. She later perjures herself in court by testifying that Lee raped her and killed Tommy. After getting away with the murder of Tommy, Popeye is executed for a killing he did not commit. Miss Drake remains a desecrated temple who found her "sanctuary" in a Memphis sporting house.

Novelist William Faulkner, whose lurid novel *Sanctuary* (1931) inspired two gangster pictures.

After *Sanctuary* was published, literary critics wondered why Paramount paid $6,000 for the screen rights to the novel in the spring of 1932.[4] The reason is not far to seek: Paramount had filmed Ernest Hemingway's *A Farewell to Arms* in 1932, and it became the top grosser of the year. The Hays Office was concerned about the filming of *Sanctuary*, however, and James Wingate, one of Hays's right-hand men, reminded Paramount that the Hemingway script had been heavily censored. Wingate met with Paramount officials and advised the studio to "make a Sunday school story" out of the book.[5] Moreover, Paramount was further advised that they should change the name of the film so that it would not be associated with Faulkner's notorious novel. Accordingly, the movie was entitled *The Story of Temple Drake*, "based on a novel by William Faulkner."[6]

Screenwriter Oliver Garrett sought to turn out a screenplay that would be acceptable to Hays. For example, Trigger (the Popeye character in the book) is not impotent in the film, so he does not use a grotesque artificial means to violate Temple. Furthermore, in the movie, Garrett supplies a bona fide love interest for Temple by having Stephen Benbow (Horace Benbow in the novel), Lee's lawyer, carry a torch for Temple in the picture.

In the opening scene, Judge Drake (Sir Guy Standing) tells the admirable young attorney that he wishes that his granddaughter Temple would become interested in someone like him. Stephen (William Gargan) replies that he has tried unsuccessfully to win Temple's affections.

Once Wingate approved Garrett's revised screenplay, Paramount proceeded to cast the film. The studio chose Jack La Rue, a rising young actor, to play Trigger. For the role of Temple, the studio selected Miriam Hopkins, who had scored a personal triumph in Ernst Lubitsch's *Trouble in Paradise* (1932). The director was Stephen Roberts, whose films, like the Ronald Colman vehicle *The Man Who Broke the Bank at Monte Carlo* (1938), were "entertaining but insignificant."[7] Finally, the director of photography for *The Story of Temple Drake* was Karl Struss, who had won an Oscar as cocinematographer on F. W. Murnau's *Sunrise* (1927).

In March 1933, James Wingate and Joseph Breen, who would replace Will Hays in less than a year, had a private screening of the movie. Breen filed a report with Hays that denounced the picture, warning that it would bring down on the Hays Office the "wrathful condemnation of decent people everywhere."[8] Hays decided to reject the film out of hand.

In addition, the New York State Censor Board informed Hays that they planned to ban the movie.

Hays called a meeting with Paramount executives and the New York Censor Board. They agreed on cuts in the film that produced a release print that they could approve for exhibition. They had chopped the movie down to seventy-one minutes—less than the running time of a mainstream feature film. *The Story of Temple Drake* was released in May 1933.

In the movie, Judge Drake is Temple's grandfather, rather than her father, as in the novel, to explain why he is so ineffectual in his efforts to control Temple's behavior. Roberts begins one scene with a close-up of a grandfather clock, showing the late hour. Then the camera pans to Temple entering the front door after a date. The judge confronts Temple on the stairs about her late hours, and a portrait hanging by the staircase of one of the family's female ancestors frowns in disapproval of Temple's behavior. A later scene shows Judge Drake's housekeeper (Hattie McDaniel) examining a torn piece of Temple's lingerie as she quips, "If Judge Drake did the laundry he'd know more about Miss Temple." Another scene depicts Stephen reading a bawdy verse about Temple scrawled on a men's room wall before he erases it in disgust and disbelief.

The sequence of events in the Old Frenchman's Place develops much as it does in the book. When Toddy Gowan (Gowan Stevens in the novel) leaves Temple in the lurch, Ruby (Florence Eldridge) puts her to bed. Trigger enters the room, smoking a cigarette; in the darkness, only the pinpoint glow of his cigarette as he moves across the room is needed to suggest what he is up to. Ruby turns on a lamp; banishes Trigger from the room; and hides Temple in the barn, where Tommy can guard her. The next morning, Trigger climbs a ladder to the loft above where Temple is sequestered. He lets himself down into the stall where Temple is hiding and shoots Tommy, who is her sentinel. As Trigger advances toward the camera, we hear Temple scream, and the screen goes black. Roberts and his cameraman, Karl Struss, manage to "suggest everything while showing nothing."[9]

As a matter of fact, Roberts had originally planned to portray the rape scene somewhat more directly. Assistant producer Jean Negulesco, later a director himself, recalled that that version did not pass the censor.[10] The movie dispenses with Alabama Red because Trigger is not impotent in the film. So it is with Trigger that Temple carries on an affair at Miss Reba's.

Ruby informs Stephen where Temple can be found, but Temple refuses to testify on behalf of Lee Goodwin (Irving Pichel) because she fears for her reputation. She tells Trigger she is fed up with their relationship and that she is leaving him. They quarrel, and Trigger, a cruel gangster, vows that he will never let her go. She snatches his gun from the bed and fires. As he expires, there is a close-up of his hand crushing out a cigarette in an ashtray. His dead fingers clutch her hat, and "she must pry them open to retrieve the incriminating evidence."[11] Before she testifies in court, Stephen tells Temple sympathetically but firmly, "It's your duty before God." Temple does not tell the truth on the witness stand; however, before she leaves the courtroom, she blurts out that she wants to reveal everything. And so she does, stating, "I went to the city with Trigger and stayed with him until this week." After she admits to shooting Trigger, she faints. Stephen carries her from the courtroom, saying to Judge Drake, "Be proud of her, Judge. I am."

After the picture was completed, the outcry against it continued. The industry trade paper, *Harrison Reports*, stated, "Never before have sex situations been so boldly and luridly pictured."[12] On the other hand, *Time* published a positive review, saying that Jack La Rue was "effectively sinister," and that Miriam Hopkins "gave a brilliant performance as Temple." *Time* concluded that Stephen Roberts had managed to squeeze the "last ounce of horror" from the script.[13]

The negative reputation of the movie largely continues to this day. Leslie Halliwell's *Film Guide* piece about the film still writes the movie off as a shocking gangster picture "restructured from a notorious book."[14] What's more, the film has virtually disappeared since its original release in 1933, except for scattered screenings throughout the years. William K. Everson, the distinguished film historian, held a New York screening of the movie in 1971; he pointed out to me that the picture had the dubious distinction of being the last straw that almost single-handedly initiated the crackdown by the administration of the Motion Picture Production Code, which resulted in the filming of such family classics as *David Copperfield* and *Wuthering Heights* in the later 1930s.[15] This seems somewhat surprising since the sexual abnormalities on which the movie's sordid reputation was based were mostly left out of the film's shooting script.

Stephen Roberts, who died three years after he made *The Story of Temple Drake*, deserves credit for making an honest and thought-provoking

Jack La Rue plays a gangster who kidnaps a rich girl in two gangster films, here with Miriam Hopkins in *The Story of Temple Drake* (1933); he also appears in *No Orchids for Miss Blandish* (1948).

film. Indeed, in 2012, *Sight and Sound* declared that *The Story of Temple Drake* is "still a fascinating film" today.[16] Still, at the time of the film's release, there were complaints in some quarters that the movie condoned Temple's shooting of Trigger, even though as one film history states, "this one was as condonable a murder as ever was."[17]

In 1934, Joseph Ignatius Breen was appointed industry censor with a mandate to press the studios to adhere to the Motion Picture Production Code. The strict enforcement of the code and curbing of the production of gangster movies initiated by *Little Caesar* motivated the founding of the Catholic Legion of Decency that same year. Perhaps Nick Pinkerton said it best when he wrote, "With the ascent of Joseph I. Breen to the czardom of the Production Code Administration, the Hays Code of 1930 finally became the enforced law of Hollywood in the summer of 1934."[18]

It is a matter of record that James Hadley Chase's lurid novel *No Orchids for Miss Blandish* was heavily indebted to *Sanctuary* for its plot. The affinity of the two novels was further underscored when *No Orchids for*

Miss Blandish was filmed in 1948, and Jack La Rue was cast once more in the role of the gangster modeled on Faulkner's Popeye. Made in England, like *The Story of Temple Drake*, the movie caused quite a scandal.

No Orchids for Miss Blandish (1948)

British crime novelist James Hadley Chase (pen name for Rene Raymond) wrote *No Orchids for Miss Blandish* in 1939, with a dictionary of American slang and a copy of James M. Cain's *The Postman Always Rings Twice* open on his desk. In 1944, George Orwell wrote that the novel "seems to have enjoyed its greatest popularity in 1940, during the Battle of Britain and the Blitz." It helped to take people's minds off being bombed by the Nazis. Orwell judged the book to be a slavish imitation of such American pulp fiction authors as Cain. Nevertheless, he found it a good read, "with hardly a wasted word."[19] As critic John Aldridge said of Faulkner's fiction—with *Sanctuary* in mind—Faulkner "somehow managed to produce several of the most anguished and subversive literary masterpieces of the twentieth century."[20] Chase's book is clearly an imitation of Faulkner's better novel.

A stage version of *No Orchids for Miss Blandish* was produced in London, in 1942, with Linden Travers in the title role, and it was well received, probably because, as a rule, theatergoers are more sophisticated than the mass audiences who go to movies. So there were no protests about the play. George Minter, head of Renown Films, a movie distribution company, decided to advance into the field of film production and picked *No Orchids for Miss Blandish* as his first project. The script, which was composed by the film's director, St. John Clowes, was approved by the British Board of Film Censors (BBFC), after some revisions. By 1948, a "more liberal policy toward gangster films had emerged in postwar Britain." As a result, the script seemed no more brutal to the BBFC than that of the average gangster movie.[21]

George Minter picked St. John Clowes to help the picture. A journeyman director, Clowes had directed his first film in 1928, and continued making low-budget second features. He was pleased that Minter had given him a bigger budget than he was accustomed to for his bargain basement films.[22] Linden Travers was slated to repeat her role as Miss Blandish, which she had played on the stage, and Jack La Rue was recreating the gangster character he had played in *The Story of Temple Drake*.

The present film is set in New York, in 1948, the year it was produced. The largely British cast had to struggle with speaking lines peppered with American slang. But the American setting is important, as Dave Kehr points out: "Clowes had cleverly transposed England's rigid class structure" to New York, "where the rules of class relations can be thrillingly violated," with an aristocratic woman falling in love with a lower-class man.[23] Several English critics noted that the movie attempted to imitate an "American-style gangster melodrama," a bit more slick than a British crime movie.[24]

Many of the British reviews of the movie were filled with outrage. The *Monthly Film Bulletin*, published by the British Film Institute, took the picture to task for being an "exhibition of brutality, perversion, sex, and sadism. With pseudo-American accents the actors battle their way through a script laden with suggestive dialogue." The film was even denounced on the floor of the British Parliament for being indecent and immoral.[25]

Richard Gordon, Minter's representative in the United States, reported to him that the Breen Office (formerly the Hays Office) turned thumbs down on the picture. Gordon reminded Breen that the stage version of *No Orchids for Miss Blandish* had been well reviewed in 1942, as a "good gangster play."[26] In reply, Breen stated that the Motion Picture Production Code declared that, "Everything possible in a play is not possible in a film," because motion pictures command a mass audience of all ages.[27] In essence, what Breen was saying was that movies are fundamentally a family medium. Hence, only films suitable for the entire family should be produced. But no tampering with *No Orchids for Miss Blandish* could make it family fare.

The Legion of Decency assigned the movie a condemned rating. They explained that when one reads the novel, one can sift the words through one's imagination and filter out as much of the unpleasantness as one cares to, but you cannot do this when you are looking at the film. Miss Blandish (who is not given a first name in either the book or the film) is a frustrated woman who renounces the restricted life she has lived in her father's house and seeks satisfaction with a gangster. That was unacceptable to the guardians of morality. Indeed, Gordon bickered with the New York State Censor Board for two years about deletions in the film before it was released in New York. The original, uncut version was at long last released on DVD in 2010.[28]

The movie opens with a shot of the New York skyline to tip the viewer off that the picture takes place in the United States. An orchid corsage is delivered to the Blandish mansion for the heroine, and she instructs the maid to refuse it, saying, "No orchids for Miss Blandish." The corsage was sent to her by Slim Grisson, the boss of the Grisson mob (Jack La Rue). He is infatuated with Miss Blandish (Linden Travers).

Miss Blandish is subsequently kidnapped and sequestered in a cabin in the woods. Slim tells her he is not interested in collecting a ransom, but in having a sexual liaison with her. He then transfers her to the Black Dice Club, where he has a private suite; it is a gambling casino run by his mob. As time goes on, they fall in love, and "Slim begins to think that he should let her go"; but she refuses to leave him, explaining that he is the first "real man" that she has met. Kehr comments, "Clowes tones down Chase's graphic sadomasochism into an almost . . . conventional romance."[29] They return to the cabin in the woods, where they make love in front of a roaring fire, which, of course, symbolizes their overheated passion.

Slim's mother objects to his love affair because "women make trouble." But Slim has a showdown with her at the Black Dice Club, and his mother relents. Brian McFarlane writes, "There is a striking anticipation of Raoul Walsh's *White Heat* (1949) in the idea of a gangster with a dominant mother"[30] (see chapter 5). Fenner, a private detective enraged by Miss Blandish's father, tracks her to Slim's cabin and leads the police there. Slim tells Miss Blandish that the time they have had together is all the happiness he could expect from this life. "We just never got the breaks," he declares. With that, Slim goes outside and deliberately shoots at the police to force them to return fire and kill him. "I'll be seeing you," Blandish mutters. Fenner takes her back to her father's house, where she commits suicide by hurling herself out of a window. She was convinced that life without Slim would be intolerable. As she lies dead on the pavement with a corsage of orchids next to her, pedestrians walk by and crush the corsage, indicating how her hopes for a fulfilling love life have been crushed. (The passersby do not seem to be bothered by a corpse on the sidewalk!)

The outcry against the movie in England was repeated in the American press. Gordon remembers an article in *Life* magazine about the film's premiere in London entitled "London Can't Take It." This is a reference to a wartime documentary about the Blitz entitled "London Can Take It."

That is to say that the Brits could stand the Blitz, but not *No Orchids for Miss Blandish*. Yet, the movie is a serious work, worthy of the attention of discerning filmgoers, a thought-provoking gangster film. Still, to this day, the film continues to have a controversial reputation. In the *Film Guide*, Halliwell calls it an "awful gangster movie from a bestselling shocker."[31] Linden Travers hazarded that one reason the film was castigated by U.S. critics was that the antihero was a hardened criminal; "that was unusual at the time."[32] Suffice it to say that *The Story of Temple Drake* and *No Orchids for Miss Blandish* are two gangster pictures that deserve the kind of reassessment I have accorded them here.

DEAD END AND *THIS GUN FOR HIRE*

Dead End (1937)

Robert Warshow states in "The Gangster as Tragic Hero" that the gangster is "what we want to be or what we are afraid we will become."[1] That observation certainly sums up *Dead End*, the first film in which Humphrey Bogart played a gangster to perfection. The picture picked up on a theme in *The Public Enemy* and developed it further: "The bad kids grow up to be bad adults, and the Dead End Kids are at a similar risk in *Dead End*."[2]

Sidney Kingsley's social protest drama *Dead End* opened at the Belasco Theater on Broadway in October 1935, to rave reviews for a successful run of sixty-five weeks. The film's director, William Wyler (*Dodsworth*), saw the play in March 1936, and prevailed upon independent producer Sam Goldwyn to buy the screen rights for him. Wyler was particularly impressed by the elaborate set that designer Norman Bel Geddes had constructed for the play: a "narrow tenement street dead-ended at the East River and ran up against a swanky new high rise."[3] Gregory Black adds,

> A sturdy masonry wall, guarded by a row of spikes on top, separates the wealthy residents of the East River Terrace apartment building from the squalid tenement buildings that line the other side of the street. The lives of the characters are determined by which side of the spiked wall they live on.[4]

A gangster, Baby Face Martin, a boss in the New York underworld, comes back for a visit to his old neighborhood. The members of the local youth gang, led by Tommy Gordon, idolize Martin. Tommy is being raised by his older sister Drina, who has little control of the boy. He inevitably gets into trouble with the law. The final curtain falls with Tommy probably headed for reform school, where he might well grow up to be the next Baby Face Martin. Indeed, the chief concern of the play, and the film derived from it, is that the rebellious, delinquent boys in the slums will grow up to be gangsters. Pauline Kael endorsed the play because it "radiates the Broadway social consciousness of the 1930s."[5]

Goldwyn entrusted the screenplay of *Dead End* to playwright and screenwriter Lillian Hellman. Joseph Breen, the film industry censor, advised Goldwyn that the movie should be less emphatic than the play in "showing the contrast between the conditions of the poor in tenements and the rich in apartment houses." Hellman remembered Goldwyn instructing her to "clean up the play," but what he really meant was to "cut off its balls."[6]

But Hellman managed to retain the play's social consciousness in her script. Drina Gordon, Tommy's older sister, is committed to social action that will provide a better life for her and Tommy, without getting involved with such underworld types as Baby Face Martin. Drina, writes Mike Cormack, "as a socially committed heroine, is without equal in 1930s Hollywood."[7]

"In 1937," William Wyler told me,

> I filmed Sidney Kingsley's play *Dead End*, which dealt with kids growing up in the New York slums. I asked Sam Goldwyn if I could make the film in New York, because the background was so integral to the plot. But he said, "I'll build you a pier on the East River and some tenements right here on a Hollywood sound stage." Everyone marveled at the huge waterfront set, which was constructed as the principal setting of the film, but to me it looked very phony and artificial. I heard later that *Dead End* was instrumental in getting new legislation to clean up the slums in New York City, because these kids needed better surroundings to grow up in.

Some of the reviews raised this point. "That was a pleasant surprise to me, because the slums depicted in the film never looked like the real thing to me," Wyler concluded.[8]

William Wyler, director of *Dead End* (1937), at the time the author interviewed him.

Few critics agreed with Wyler that the film's gigantic riverfront set, designed by Richard Day, looked artificial; in fact, several reviewers praised its authentic look. Charles Afron observes that the Broadway origins of the property are not disguised in a film like *Dead End*. "Instead they are made into a virtue."[9] The action of the film takes place in one central waterfront setting. During filming, Wyler extended the action principally by staging it throughout the slum tenement, from the

basement to the roof. The constant movement between the various playing areas kept the movie from becoming static.

After the opening credits, which are painted on traffic signs, the
movie opens with a printed prologue:

> Every street in New York ends in a river. For many years the dirty banks
> of the East River were lined with the tenements of the poor. Then the
> rich, discovering that the river traffic was picturesque, moved their
> houses eastward. And now the terraces of these great apartment houses
> look down into the windows of the tenements.

The film proper begins with a panoramic shot of the New York skyline, after which the camera pans to the waterfront below. Finally, the
camera zeroes in on the film's elaborate principal setting, a slum street
that comes to a dead end at the waterfront. A luxury apartment building
has been erected where the slum frontage has been cleared, so that the
apartment complex adjoins a tawdry tenement on the waterfront. The
film's action takes place in and around the towering rental apartment
building and its neighboring slum dwelling. Edith Lee calls this slum
tenement one of the seediest sets in Hollywood history. Richard Day's
expression of poverty includes "every crack in the wall, thick coats of dust,
peeling paint, and stairways that creak."[10]

The tenement is where the members of a local juvenile gang live. As
the camera explores the narrow corridors and cramped living quarters,
the viewer gets a sense of the confinement that the boys who live there
must endure. This slum dwelling is what Michael Anderegg terms a
"labyrinthine trap."[11] Moreover, the tenement is located on a dead-end
street, which symbolizes how the boys have already reached a dead end;
that is, they have no prospects for a promising future. Underscoring this
point, Black writes that it is clear that the kids "have little education and
no skills and are destined to live in the slums; only a miracle will save
them from a life of crime."[12]

That is why, Black continues, Joseph Breen, the industry censor,
stressed that this film offered a strong plea for the elimination of the
slums as a means of crime prevention. In fact, the ads for the picture aptly
referred to "Dead End, cradle of crime." Carl Rollyson comments that
Lillian Hellman was praised by most reviewers of the film for "producing
a taut script" that retained much of the play's unvarnished realism.[13]

A former inhabitant of the riverfront tenement, Baby Face Martin (Humphrey Bogart) comes back for a nostalgic visit to his old stomping grounds. He is a notorious figure in the New York underworld, and the members of the youth gang revere him. "He is the future, as far as these youngsters are concerned," writes Graham Greene; furthermore, Martin's early life as a juvenile delinquent growing up in this grubby neighborhood "is there before your eyes in the juvenile gangsters."[14]

Martin has come home to see his mother and old girlfriend. His meeting with both women proves to be a disaster. He spies his mother (Marjorie Main) from a distance and "calls after her excitedly," says James Neibaur, "like a child with a good report card."[15] "Mom!" he shouts as he runs toward her. Her hostile response to his greeting is to slap him soundly across the face as she spits out her words at him: "Don't call me Mom!" She tells him in no uncertain terms that she despises him and everything he stands for, and then she angrily turns her back on him and stalks away.

His meeting with Francie (Claire Trevor), his erstwhile girlfriend, is equally painful for him. He happens upon her on the street and invites her

Humphrey Bogart (left) and Billy Halop (center) with the Dead End Kids in *Dead End* (1937). This is Bogart's definitive performance of a gangster.

to rekindle their old relationship by coming away with him. She replies pathetically, "Look at me good—I'm not what I used to be." Francie steps out of the dark doorway in which she has been standing and into the sunlight. Mike Cormack writes that Gregg Toland lights Francie in a "harsh and unflattering" way at this point. The glaring light of day mercilessly exposes her as the shabby, diseased prostitute she has become. Although there is no direct reference to Francie's advanced case of venereal disease, only a young and naïve moviegoer would fail to infer what she suffers from. With deep revulsion, Martin slips her a few bills and turns away from her, as his mother had turned away from him. Hunk (Alan Jenkins), Martin's sidekick, who has accompanied him on his trip to the old neighborhood, advises Martin, in the wake of his two bitter confrontations with the past, "Never go back; always go forward."

Bogart's handling of the two aforementioned scenes are reason enough to justify the critical opinion that in *Dead End* Bogart gives one of his finest performances as a gangster. Bogart skillfully suggests that this gangster's tough exterior hides a sensitivity that yearns for the love both of his mother and his old flame. Martin's sole satisfaction while he is back in the old neighborhood is to bask in the adulation of the gang of tough kids on the block, who admire him for making good in the rackets uptown.

Tommy (Billy Halop), the ringleader of the gang, looks up to Martin more than the others do. Thus, Tommy, in particular, takes to heart Martin's advice to always carry a knife, since, as Martin says, "You never know when you will have to use it." Consequently, when Mr. Griswald, the father of a rich boy who lives in the nearby luxury apartment building, confronts Tommy for roughing up his son, Tommy pulls a penknife on him, grazes his hand with it, and gets away from him. Drina (Sylvia Sidney), Tommy's sister, who constitutes the only family he has, is distraught when she learns that her kid brother is being pursued by the police at Mr. Griswald's behest.

Two scenes in the movie at this juncture are noteworthy for Wyler's use of visual imagery. There is, first of all, the scene in which Tommy cowers in a shadowy cellar stairway as he hides from the cops. As Cormack observes, Wyler shows us "Tommy's face in close-up, crushed by the shadow of the prisonlike bars of the stairway railing."[16] This image implies that Tommy is already imprisoned by his wretched life in the cruel and indifferent world of the slums.

Another scene in which Wyler's visual knack stands out is that in which Dave Connell (Joel McCrea), Drina's boyfriend, has a confrontation with Martin in an alley while Hunk is standing by. Dave warns the mobster to stay away from the neighborhood kids because of his bad influence on them. The pair get into a scuffle; Martin then pulls a gun on Dave and retreats down the alley. Dave, in turn, grabs Hunk's gun and pursues Martin up a fire escape. Dave fires upward at Martin, who falls into the alley below, where he soon dies. The image of Martin's ignominious fall from the top of the fire escape to the ground below symbolizes that he has been knocked off the pedestal on which Tommy and his gang had placed him. Martin's downfall recalls that of Little Caesar and Tom Powers in *The Public Enemy*.

When Martin's mother discovers that he is dead, she screams in anguish—she really did love her son. The leader of the police squad, who shows up after Dave kills Martin, is played by Thomas Jackson, who had a similar role in *Little Caesar*. Here he reassures Dave that he will get the reward for bringing down a public enemy. As the film draws to a close, Dave promises Drina that he will bail Tommy out of jail with the reward money, since Martin had a price on his head. He will use the money to save Tommy from going to reform school.

But the movie's final scene implies that the rest of Tommy's gang will not be so lucky. As the boys disappear into a dark alley in long shot, Wyler photographs them through a fence, reminding the viewer once again that these delinquent boys are imprisoned in the harsh, grim world of the slums (the cradle of crime). They remain convinced that they must stick together in their gang to survive.

Novelist and screenwriter Graham Greene, who was also a film critic, describes *Dead End* as a "magnificent picture of the environment that breeds the gangster."[17] By the same token, Joseph Breen emphasized that the film offered a "strong plea for slum elimination," so that youngsters can grow into mature and decent citizens.[18] The movie was also endorsed by the Catholic Legion of Decency in similar terms. What's more, *Dead End* was nominated for an Academy Award as Best Picture, an honor accorded to no other gangster picture up to that time. In addition, Claire Trevor, Gregg Toland, and Richard Day were also nominated for Oscars. Although none of them won, it was still a stellar showing.

It is interesting to note, as a footnote to the film, that Tommy and the other members of his gang were referred to in publicity layouts for the movie as the Dead End Kids, even though they are never called that in the movie itself. The young actors who played the gang members continued to be billed as the Dead End Kids in the films they made together after *Dead End* for the next couple of years in an effort to cash in on the huge success of the movie. They costarred with James Cagney, for example, in *Angels with Dirty Faces* (1938). The title of the later movie is actually a reference to the boys singing a snatch of "If I Had the Wings of an Angel" in *Dead End*, implying their wish to escape from their prisonlike ghetto.

Billy Halop broke away from the group in the early 1940s, with the hope of building a career as an actor, but he failed to do so. The rest of the group continued as the East Side Kids (1940–1945), and then as the Bowery Boys (1946–1958), in a series of low-budget second features as they became "aging delinquents." Halop and the others gave their best performances in *Dead End*. Indeed, they never recaptured the "vibrancy and sheer animal spirits they exhibited for Wyler."[19]

It is significant to note that Greene, when he was a film critic in the 1930s in London, praised *Dead End*. In 1942, an American film, *This Gun for Hire*, based on a Greene novel, was released by Paramount. Alan Ladd plays Raven, a cold, hardened killer who is much like Baby Face Martin. "Gangster films began turning very dark" in the late 1930s, according to film historians Gerald Mast and Bruce Kawin, with movies like *Dead End* concentrating on the "inevitability of crime in urban America, and on criminals who were not simply selfish and tough like Little Caesar," but downright pathological, like Raven in *This Gun for Hire*.[20]

Greene published the novel *A Gun for Sale* in England, in 1936; it was published in the United States in the same year as *This Gun for Hire*. Paramount produced a film version in Hollywood under the same name in 1942.

This Gun for Hire (1942)

Greene's book is about a contract killer named James Raven, who has a harelip that both physically symbolizes the spiritual deformity of his personality and helps one to understand the morbid loneliness that has driven him to become an embittered assassin. Because of his wretched childhood in a reformatory, Raven is obsessed with the notion that no one can be trusted, and he is convinced that betrayal lurks at every corner. Even looking at a cheap Nativity scene in the lobby of a fleabag hotel reminds him that the little plaster child in its mother's arms is waiting for the "double-cross, the whips, the nails." As Raven says to an onlooker, "They put him on the spot, eh? . . . You see, I know the whole story; I'm educated."[21] Professor Samuel Hynes comments, "The baby in the crèche manger will grow up to be betrayed by a friend. . . . Betrayal and cruelty are realities in Raven's world."[22]

In the 1936 novel, Raven is hired by an enemy agent to murder a government minister of an unnamed country and thus help to instigate a war. The agent, however, then betrays Raven to the police to get him out of the way, once the job has been accomplished. In the course of his fleeing from the police, Raven meets a girl whom he finally brings himself to trust, only to have her turn him in to her fiancé, who has been in charge of the manhunt for Raven all along. After a gun battle, Raven dies, so disillusioned with this life that he does not fear what will come next, which he hopes will be better than the present life.

The screenplay for *This Gun for Hire* was cowritten by W. R. Burnett, whose novel *Little Caesar* was the basis of the classic gangster picture. Several changes were introduced into the script to make the plot more relevant for wartime America during World War II. The setting was changed from England in the 1930s to California in the 1940s, where fifth columnists are selling secret formulas to Japan. Moreover, Judith Adamson opines, "Raven has a crippled wrist in his coat pocket. The wrist was an unfortunate substitute for the original Raven's harelip, because it drastically reduced the hero's psychological complexity."[23]

Paramount chose Frank Tuttle to direct *This Gun for Hire*—not surprisingly since, as I have written elsewhere, Tuttle was a dependable filmmaker who had directed movies in a variety of genres, including such glossy thrillers as the original 1935 version of Dashiell Hammett's *Glass Key*, with George Raft. David Thomson's assessment of Tuttle is that "none of his films have survived as more than typical studio product."[24] Except for *This Gun for Hire*, *Glass Key* is arguably his finest achievement. Brian Baxter notes that *This Gun for Hire* is "one of Hollywood's great, underrated thrillers. . . . The movie is brisk, well-acted, atmospheric, and always entertaining."[25]

For years, Alan Ladd had been stuck in bit parts in films, for example, as a reporter in the last sequence of *Citizen Kane*, until he was selected to play Raven opposite Veronica Lake (*Sullivan's Travels*). At five feet, five inches tall, Ladd had a perfect match in Lake, who was five feet, two inches tall. Furthermore, they had an on-screen chemistry that made them a box-office sensation. Tuttle managed to commandeer an experienced cinematographer, John Seitz, who had photographed Valentino's breakout movie, *The Four Horsemen of the Apocalypse* (1921). Seitz was well known for creating a sinister atmosphere of tension and dread with menacing, shadowy lighting. This knack would come in handy for the present film.

"The film got off to a good start," Greene remembered, "but then the heroine was introduced as a female conjurer working for the FBI, and that had nothing to do with my story."[26] The movie does indeed get off to a good start. In the opening scene, Ladd establishes Raven's combination of boyish charm and unflinching cruelty. The movie begins in a tawdry San Francisco hotel room, "with Raven caressing a stray kitten and then slapping down the chambermaid, who was foolish enough to throw the cat out." In a single scene, Ladd portrays a kind of gangster not seen in a Hollywood film before: a "remorseless killer with charm and sex appeal."[27]

Graham Greene, author of the novel on which the movie *This Gun for Hire* (1942) is based.

Raven keeps a rendezvous with Albert Baker (Frank Ferguson), an American scientist who is selling government secrets to Raven's employer, who, in turn, is peddling them to the Japanese. After Raven takes the secret documents, there is a glint in his eye as he reaches into his briefcase and pulls out not the money that the scientist expects, but a gun, with which he summarily shoots Baker. Now there is no question of Baker blackmailing Raven's employer. Raven notices the dead man's mistress and mutters, "You weren't supposed to be here." In a panic, she slams the bedroom door in his face, and he shoots her through the door. He hears her body fall to the floor on the other side of the door. As Raven leaves the building, we momentarily get a glimpse of the more humane side of his personality, which he is always striving to suppress, by watching him retrieve a crippled child's ball for her. "He is about to kill her," Jack Nolan points out, "since she is the only witness who can place him at the scene, but he does not."[28]

Later he briefly refers to his miserable childhood as an orphan. He had lived in a foster home with his aunt, who tried to "beat the bad blood" out of him. One day she branded his wrist with a red-hot flat iron, and he stabbed her to death. Because of his unhappy childhood, Raven believes that no one can be trusted, but that is as close as the movie comes to probing Raven's character in the manner in which Greene does in the novel. Raven decides to move on to Los Angeles once the enemy agent who hired him turned him in to the cops. On the night train to L.A., he meets Ellen Graham (Veronica Lake), a female magician appearing in a revue in L.A. He dares to trust her, and she develops some feelings for him. She happens to be the girlfriend of Lieutenant Michael Crane (Robert Preston), the detective who is pursuing Raven. Accordingly, she is torn between turning him in to the police and shielding a murderer.

The movie is a fine chase melodrama, but the two songs that Ellen sings as part of her magic act are completely out of keeping with the tone of the film. Furthermore, the added complication of Ellen's working for the FBI as a lady spy makes no contribution to the film, unless it is to back up the patriotic appeal that Ellen makes at one point to Raven about his collusion with fifth columnists: "This war is everybody's business, yours too," she concludes. Raven calls her speech "flag waving." Willard Gates (Laird Cregar) is backing the revue Ellen is appearing in; he is also the "Man Friday" of Alvin Brewster, the arms manufacturer; Gates is the middleman between Raven and Brewster. Gates hired Raven to kill Albert Baker. The unscrupulous Brewster orders Gates to pay off Raven with marked bills so he can be apprehended by the police. Brewster, the cruel, aging industrialist, is played by Tully Marshall (*Queen Kelly*). Raven, seeking revenge on Gates and Brewster, shadows Gates to Brewster's office at the munitions plant. When Raven draws a bead on Brewster, the old man succumbs to a heart attack; Raven aims his gun at Gates and wipes him out. Lieutenant Crane shows up in Brewster's office, accompanied by Ellen Graham, and fires on Raven. He expires with a "little-boy smile" on his face, asking Ellen with his last breath, "Did I do alright for you?"[29] He is referring to the fact that Gates had planned to have her exterminated because she knew too much about his involvement with Raven and the fifth columnists. Now Gates is out of the picture.

Despite its departures from Greene's novel, *This Gun for Hire* is a good picture in many ways, and it prompted film critic Philips Hartung to say, "With all the changes in the story, the Greene original still survives. The tense excitement of the novel and its cold violence are natural cinema material. What readers of the novel will miss principally is Greene's expertly

Alan Ladd in his career-making role as the hired killer in *This Gun for Hire* (1942).

interwoven asides on the morality of this study of evil."[30] Indeed, one also misses the haunting psychological dimension of the book. In the movie, there are few references to Raven's background. Nor does Alan Ladd have a harelip, as Raven does in the book; as a result, we do not understand Raven's motivation for being so cynical and pessimistic to the extent that we do in the novel, but he does come across as deeply disturbed.

In actual fact, Alan Ladd gave a fascinating performance as Raven, which catapulted him to stardom and made the film a superior gangster picture. Tuttle rounded out his career with *Hell on Frisco Bay* (1955), a gangster movie in which he paired Edward G. Robinson and Alan Ladd, photographed by John Seitz. With *This Gun for Hire*, Tuttle can be credited with introducing a new strain into the American gangster genre: the criminal who is not only violent and corrupt, but emotionally disturbed as well. One can draw a straight line from Raven as a mental case in *This Gun for Hire* to Richard Widmark's maniacal gangster in *The Kiss of Death* (1947) to James Cagney's pathological mobster in *White Heat* (1949) and beyond.

CRISS CROSS AND *WHITE HEAT*

Since Germany was the foremost center of filmmaking in Europe by 1920, Austrians like Fritz Lang worked in Berlin movie studios alongside such native Germans as Robert Siodmak. Lang joined the exodus to Hollywood in 1933, after Hitler nationalized the German film industry, but Siodmak made movies in France throughout the 1930s and only went to Hollywood in 1939, when World War II broke out in Europe.

"The rise of Nazism and the coming of World War II had driven such important crime-film directors" as Robert Siodmak and Fritz Lang to the United States.[1] By then, the milieu of gangster film had become a darker place, both psychologically and morally, as movies like *Dead End* and *This Gun for Hire* indicate. The gangster chose violence as a weapon against the brutal hardness of a "decaying society."[2]

Some of the gangster movies of the period belonged to the class of American films christened film noir (dark film) by postwar French critics. Siodmak brought with him from his years in Berlin studios his "mastery of shadowy lighting and worked with cinematographers with a gift of extreme contrasts of light and darkness." In his peak period in Hollywood, he directed ten extraordinary film noirs in Hollywood.[3]

Criss Cross (1949)

The dark, menacing atmosphere of *Criss Cross*, coupled with the somber vision of life reflected in this tale of obsession and murder, mark this movie as film noir, as well as a gangster picture—as noted earlier, there is no reason why the same film cannot be both. The pessimistic view of life exhibited in noir movies—itself an outgrowth of the disillusionment spawned by World War II, a disillusionment that would continue into \ the period of uncertainty known as the Cold War that was the war's aftermath—is evident in *Criss Cross*, probably Siodmak's best noir. Molly Haskell describes noir movies as "those harsh and livid little tales reeking of European fatalism."[4]

Also in keeping with the conventions of film noir is the movie's air of spare, unvarnished realism, typified by the stark, documentary-like quality of the cinematography, especially the grim scenes that take place at night. Furthermore, *Criss Cross* demonstrates Siodmak's ability to create depth of character, in this instance in a movie about a faithless hussy and a naïve chump.

Siodmak attracted a first-class group of collaborators for *Criss Cross*. The intricate screenplay was by novelist and screenwriter Daniel Fuchs; Frank (née Franz) Planer, another veteran of the German film industry, was the cinematographer, an artist who, like Siodmak, favored location shooting. The musical score was composed by the Hungarian émigré to Hollywood, Miklós Rózsa, who had worked with Siodmak on *The Killers* (1946). In *Criss Cross*, his score is characterized by "unsentimental themes, driving rhythms . . . and a raw urban power" that complement the realistic look of the movie.[5]

Burt Lancaster, who plays Steve Thompson in the film, also plays the lead in *The Killers*; he perfectly embodied the vulnerability of the noir antihero. Steve is victimized by the femme fatale (fatal female), another staple of film noir—a seductive, remorseless woman who uses men and then discards them. Yvonne De Carlo plays Anna, the femme fatale and the lady for whom Steve gets involved in an armed robbery.

Franz Planer acted as location scout and chose exteriors throughout Los Angeles; for example, a house in the run-down Bunker Hill section that served as the family homestead of Steve's mother (Edna Holland) and younger brother Slade (Richard Long). There is also an old apartment building that has a faded, deteriorated look, where a small-time mob holds its meetings.

Since the term *film noir* was not in general use in Hollywood in those days, and would not be for another few years, Siodmak considered *Criss*

Cross a gangster movie. He described the antihero of a gangster picture as someone "who has failed in life and has therefore committed a crime. . . . If you give such a person a good enough motive for the crime," the audience will be on his side. This sums up the character played by Lancaster in *Criss Cross*.[6]

The title of the film is easily explained: When a person double-crosses someone who has already double-crossed them, it is called a "criss cross." The main character in Lang's movie *Scarlet Street*, which is about a criss cross, is, in fact, named Chris Cross.

The movie begins with the camera swooping down on a nightclub parking lot at night, while Steve and Anna are kissing. Their embrace is revealed by the headlights of a passing automobile. The story begins on the night before the armed robbery in which Steve is participating. Then Steve narrates, voice-over on the sound track, the events leading up to the heist. "What happened was in the cards—it was Fate," Steve asserts more than once, in a futile attempt to shirk any responsibility for what took place.

The extended flashback begins eight months earlier, when Steve comes back to town after traveling around the country, attempting to get over his divorce from Anna. They were only married for seven months, but Steve still carries a torch for her. He bunks in his mother's house in the Bunker Hill area of Los Angeles. He goes to the Rondo Club, where he and Anna used to hang out, aware that he will probably run into her there. He comments in a voice-over, "A man eats an apple, gets a piece of the core stuck between his teeth. . . . I knew one way or the other; somehow I would wind up seeing her that night." And so he does. Indeed, he becomes infatuated with her all over again. "It was in the cards," he insists, "it was Fate."

Steve's sexual enslavement to Anna is painfully obvious in the scene in which he watches her dancing to an overheated Latin American tune with another man (a young Tony Curtis). Steve's fatal attraction to his ex-wife is demonstrated vividly in this scene. One of the customers assumes that Steve is miserable about being an unlucky gambler and says to him, "You shouldn't bet if you can't afford to lose."

Steve subsequently discovers that Anna has married Slim Dundee (Dan Duryea), a second-rate racketeer, but Steve's passionate affair with Anna continues. One afternoon Slim, who suspects that Anna is

Yvonne De Carlo and Burt Lancaster in Robert Siodmak's *Criss Cross* (1949); Lancaster plays the ex-husband of De Carlo, who is unaware that she has taken up with a gangster.

two-timing him, interrupts a tryst between her and Steve. To mollify Slim, Steve, who has gotten his old job back at Horten's Armored Car Service, offers to set up an armored truck robbery involving a factory payroll. Steve hopes that his share in the loot from the armed robbery will enable him to spirit Anna away from Slim so that they can start life anew, beyond Slim's reach. With that, the forty-minute flashback ends, and the movie proceeds with the armored truck robbery.

Steve is driving the armored car when the robbery takes place. Slim's gang sets off smoke bombs when the heist commences. In the ensuing scuffle with the cops, Steve is seriously wounded by one of Slim's own men. He suddenly realizes that Slim has double-crossed him: he is meant to take the fall for the robbery. In retaliation for Slim's betrayal, Steve shoots a couple members of his mob and even wounds Slim himself. Slim gets away with half of the take from the heist. Steve later hands over the other half of the loot to Anna for safekeeping and instructs her to meet him at the cottage on the ocean that they have used as a rendezvous. Steve plans to double-cross his double-crosser: a criss cross.

Meanwhile, Steve is hospitalized with severe injuries, which the police assume he sustained in heroically attempting to foil the robbery. Mr. Nelson (Robert Osterloh, in a peerless performance) is sitting in the corridor outside of Steve's room; he is ostensibly waiting to see another patient. This harmless-looking individual, whom Steve trusts to drive him to his rendezvous with Anna, "turns out to be in Dundee's pay."[7] Nelson delivers Steve to the cottage on the shore and then inexplicably takes off. Anna is not glad to see Steve.

Anna brutally informs Steve that she plans to abscond with the loot from the payroll robbery on her own, thereby double-crossing both Slim and Steve, but Steve wants her to take him with her. She responds cruelly, "How far could I get with you? You have to take care of yourself," meaning that she cannot drag a disabled man along with her. Then she states her personal creed: "You have to do what's best for yourself. That's the kind of world it is." As a crooked politician says in Preston Sturges's film *The Great McGinty* (1940), "Everybody lives by cheating everybody else."

Nelson, of course, has tipped off Slim to the whereabouts of Steve and Anna, as Slim paid him to do. Slim suddenly materializes in the dark doorway of the cottage, carrying a cane in one hand and a gun in the other. He reassures Steve that Anna is all his and then shoots them both. They die in one another's arms, although they are obviously no Romeo and Juliet. Slim hears the police sirens blaring outside and turns away to face the cops, who followed him to the cottage of the doomed lovers.

Aside from being a superior gangster picture, *Criss Cross* also qualifies as an excellent film noir; for example, the hospital scene: "Out of the hospital darkness comes Steve's worst nightmare," Mr. Nelson, the man he thought was "harmless"—until Nelson says laconically, "You and I have a date with Dundee."[8] The shadowy setting in the hospital room suggests the sinister night world of film noir. Moreover, Siodmak's movie reflects the pessimistic and cynical view of life that is embedded in film noir. Thus, Martin Scorsese notes in his documentary *A Personal Journey through American Cinema* (1995), "There are no dispensations in film noir; you pay for your sins." Steve wanted to be with Anna again, and when they meet one last time, "it spells doom for both of them."[9]

Criss Cross was shot in 1948, and when it was released in 1949, it was not considered an exceptional movie. That is, it was not much studied or written about—until film critic Jay Cocks included it in his list of "Ten Great Movies to Be Watched Over and Over" in the mainstream magazine *TV Guide*, forty years after its release.[10] Furthermore, in *Bad Boys: The Actors of Film Noir*, Karen Burroughs Hannsberry lauds Burt Lancaster's skilled performance as an individual driven to crime to "please a lady."[11] What's more, Michael Barson anoints *Criss Cross* as "one of the best—and bleakest—noirs from that classic era."[12]

Criss Cross is finally being recognized as a top-notch gangster picture; Carlos Clarens compares it favorably to John Huston's *Asphalt Jungle*, which is an established classic (see chapter 6).[13] Thomas Leitch likens Siodmak to the other expert German directors who managed to maintain in Hollywood their expressive visual style and employ criminal plots to encapsulate a character's psychological flaws.[14] Some film historians compare Siodmak to Sternberg in this regard. Pauline Kael states that Siodmak's "swift, skillful direction makes the terror convincing" in his American movies.[15] Siodmak returned to Germany in 1954, to continue making German films for the balance of his career. In retrospect, it is evident that his American period was the peak of his output as a director. Yet, Kael laments, "Robert Siodmak's Hollywood films are much better known than he is."[16]

White Heat (1949)

Raoul Walsh, like Robert Siodmak, has never been accorded the regard he deserves as a director of crime films. Michael Atkinson believes that Walsh's filmography, like that of William Wellman, contains a number of routine features he made at the studio's behest so that his outstanding films, like *White Heat*, run the risk of being overlooked and neglected. "His best films," writes Atkinson, "are essential because of the balance [that] Walsh effortlessly attains between human frailties (doubt, weakness, woe) and the pulpy, fast-moving exigencies of popular Hollywood."[17] His lesser movies, like the Jack Benny comedy *The Horn Blows at Midnight*, are best forgotten.

Walsh started his career in movies as an actor, playing John Wilkes Booth in D. W. Griffith's *The Birth of a Nation* (1915). That same year, he directed his first gangster picture, *Regeneration*, which demonstrated what he had learned working as an apprentice to Griffith. Walsh went on to make some fine action movies during the sound period. In 1939, he joined forces with James Cagney for *The Roaring Twenties*, an important gangster picture that recalls *The Public Enemy*. Ten years later they collaborated on *White Heat*, "in which the old-style, breezy Cagney gangster had become psychotic."[18] In the original screenplay, no explanation was provided for the cruelty of the character played by Cagney, Cody Jarrett. In discussing Cody Jarrett with Walsh, Cagney asked him how they could make Cody different from the mobster that Cagney had played in *The Roaring Twenties*. According to Martin Scorsese, Walsh replied, "Let's make him crazy." Cagney chimed in, "A real psychopath."[19]

In *White Heat*, the gangster becomes a "psychologically crippled monster and a violent sadist" who is very much "on the periphery of society." In short, he becomes an "alienated social fugitive."[20] Whereas in *The Public Enemy* Tom Powers breaks his doting mother's heart, Cody Jarrett's mother is a cold-blooded, heartless woman who is the mentor of her gangster son. She encourages his criminal behavior. Ma Jarrett was modeled on the legendary Ma Barker, who presided over a mob made up of her own sons.[21]

The gangster genre had waned during World War II, when war pictures were the order of the day; with pictures like *White Heat*, it was coming back to life. Walsh surrounded Cagney with a first-class supporting cast: Margaret Wycherly, who was nominated for an Academy Award for playing Gary Cooper's mother in *Sergeant York* (1940), gives a gripping performance as Cody's insane mother. Virginia Mayo, who plays a character who cheats on her husband with Steve Cochran's character in William Wyler's *The Best Years of Our Lives* (1946), plays another two-timing wife, Verna Jarrett. This time Mayo is cheating on James Cagney,

Virginia Mayo and James Cagney in Raoul Walsh's *White Heat* (1949), the peak of Cagney's gangster movies.

once again with Steve Cochran, who has the part of Big Ed, a member of Cody's gang. Mayo is especially good as Cody's duplicitous wife. Last, but certainly not least, Robert Osterloh, the enigmatic Mr. Nelson in *Criss Cross*, is Tommy Riley, another member of Cody Jarrett's gang.

Mention should be made of the musical score by Max Steiner (*Gone with the Wind*), one of the most influential film composers of the time period. Joseph Milicia writes that Steiner's score "propels us through the film," beginning with the taut and turgid music for the opening credits, "keeping the film in high gear."[22] Joseph Breen, the industry censor, initially complained that the screenplay went into far too much detail about the planning and execution of crimes, because real criminals would find such information of practical use. The script was modified accordingly. The Catholic Legion of Decency allowed *White Heat* to squeak by with the disapproving rating "Objectionable in Part" because of what they saw as an excessive amount of violence in the picture, but the Legion of Decency's rating did not deter moviegoers from seeing *White Heat*, and the box-office returns were considerable.

White Heat starts out with a train robbery carried out by Cody Jarrett and his gang. The heist involves the killing of the two engineers in the cab of the locomotive. The gang returns to the remote cabin they use as a hideout, where Cody's mother and his wife Verna are waiting. Big Ed expresses to Verna his conviction that Cody is no longer an appropriate leader for the gang: "It ain't right having a crackpot giving orders; someone should take over." When Big Ed does take over, Verna will inevitably switch her allegiance to him.

In one scene, Cody is struck by an agonizing migraine headache that he likens to a "red-hot buzz saw" inside his head, a reference to the movie's title. Cody had faked headaches as a child to get his mother's attention; now the fancied headaches have become real. Cody and his mother retire to a bedroom. Martin Scorsese comments, "He's crying, and he sits on his mother's lap—a middle-aged man!"[23] The pathetic sight of Cody gradually sliding into his mother's lap as she comforts him, says Scorsese, emphasizes that Cody depends on his mother; she controls him. "Cody has an oedipal relationship with his mother," Drew Casper notes; "his mother never allowed him to grow up."[24]

Soon thereafter, Cody and his mob move into a cheap motel in Los Angeles. He eventually lands in prison for armed robbery—he has managed to avoid the murder charge he deserves. Cody's mother comes to see him in prison and informs him that Verna and Big Ed have been carrying on an affair since he has been in stir. His mother consoles Cody by reassuring him that the situation can be ameliorated. She says, "You'll be out soon, and then you'll be back on top of the world"—which is where his mother believes he belongs.

One day while having the noon meal in the prison mess hall, Cody receives word that his mother is dead. Given his fixation on his mother, he becomes crazed with grief. He hurls himself onto the long mess hall table, madly smashing dishes. The camera switches to an overhead shot as Cody wildly slugs the guards; he is finally subdued and jammed into a straightjacket, screaming all the while "like some mortally wounded animal."[25] The extras in the mess hall scene were not alerted to what Cagney was going to do, so their look of dismay is genuine.

Philip Evans, the Treasury agent (T-man) assigned to Cody's robbery case, arranges to have an undercover cop as Cody's cell mate, Hank Fallon, alias Nick Pardo (Edmund O'Brien). When next Cody experiences a migraine, Fallon massages his temples the way that Cody's late mother used to do. Fallon "worms his way into the confidence of his cell mate, taking over the nurturing and reassuring role of Cody's mother, despite his personal revulsion for Cody."[26] But Cody is so fond of him that he assigns to him the share of the loot from their robberies that would have gone to Cody's mother.

Cody, with the help of inmate Tommy Riley, breaks out of jail and takes Tommy and Fallon with him. He stuffs Parker, another convict, into the trunk of the getaway car because he discovers that Parker had participated in a failed attempt on Cody's life while they were in prison. When Parker complains that the trunk of the automobile is stuffy, Cody hollers, "Hold on! I'll give you some air!" Cody then riddles the trunk with bullets. Walsh was not averse to some gallows humor in the film.

Once out of jail, Cody goes after Verna and Big Ed for betraying him. He finds them in an abandoned house. Verna convinces Cody that Big Ed killed his mother so that he could take over the gang. When Cody confronts Big Ed, the latter slams a door in his face as he tries to escape Cody's wrath, but Cody shoots Ed through the closed door in the same way that Raven exterminated someone in *This Gun for Hire*. Verna, who really killed Ma Jarrett for treating her like the slut she is, reaffirms her commitment to Cody once Ed is dead.

Cody plans another robbery, this time of a chemical plant, and Fallon tips off the T-men about the caper. When the T-men, accompanied by a full complement of policemen, arrive at the plant, Cody is devastated to learn that his "buddy" Fallon is with the cops and has been betraying him from the start. Meanwhile, Verna, always the treacherous opportunist, offers to help Agent Evans take Cody alive. Nonetheless, Evans rightly sees Verna as Cody's accomplice and arrests her.

Ma Jarrett's often-repeated advice to her son, "to get to the top of the world," serves as his epitaph. Cody Jarrett's self-immolation makes for an overwhelming finale to the film. As Cody's gang members get picked off one by one by the police, he climbs to the top of a huge oil tank, laughing maniacally all the while. Fallon shoots at him with a long-range rifle, but he is not seriously wounded. "What's holding him up?" Fallon wonders. Cody, it seems, has decided to die on his own terms.

Ed Lowry's arresting description of Cody's last moments cannot be bettered: "Perched atop a refinery oil drum, engaged in a hopeless gun battle with the police, and realizing he's betrayed by Fallon, Jarrett fires his gun into the drum, shouting, 'Made it, Ma; top of the world!' The white heat explosion that follows marks Jarrett's ascension to the tragic" as he is blown into eternity.[27] The gangster as tragic hero.

White Heat marked the peak of the careers of both Raoul Walsh and James Cagney. "Walsh was the most accomplished craftsman working at Warner Bros.," and *White Heat* is his masterpiece.[28] Because Walsh's lengthy filmography contains some routine movies, he has not been given the high place in film history that he deserves. Nevertheless, there is no doubt that Raoul Walsh left an impressive body of work as his legacy.

JOHN HUSTON'S *KEY LARGO*
AND *THE ASPHALT JUNGLE*

Key Largo (1948)

In 1938, John Huston was hired as a contract screenwriter at Warner Bros., where he wrote the script for *High Sierra* (1941), a gangster movie for director Raoul Walsh and starring Humphrey Bogart. He directed *The Maltese Falcon* (1941), a superior detective movie, from his own screenplay, which was his first directorial effort, that same year. He joined the armed forces in 1942, and became a lieutenant in the Signal Corps. In 1944, Huston wrote, directed, and narrated a documentary, *The Battle of San Pietro*, and he made reference to the battle in his postwar feature *Key Largo*.

After the war, he coauthored the screenplay for *The Killers* at Universal; he was uncredited because he was under contract to Warner and could not officially work at another studio. Producer Jerry Wald persuaded him to adapt *Key Largo*, a play by Maxwell Anderson, for Warner Bros. It had opened on Broadway in November 1939, starring Paul Muni. After reading Anderson's opus carefully, Huston despaired of turning this heavy-handed, preachy antiwar play into a viable movie. It was composed in blank verse, no less. The play lasted only 105 performances on Broadway and then folded like the proverbial ninety-eight-cent card table, but Huston was committed to the project, since he was a contract director at the studio.

Anderson's play deals with King McCloud, an American who volunteers to fight for the loyalist cause against the fascists during the Spanish

Civil War (1936–1939)—not the Spanish American War, as some commentators on the play erroneously state. When McCloud sees that the loyalist cause is lost, he flees from the battlefield, but his fellow American companions-in-arms stay on and are killed. Once back in the United States, McCloud goes to visit the family of one of his dead American comrades, who run a small hotel in the Florida Keys. Some gangsters have taken control of the hotel as a hideout, and he stands up to them, losing his life in the bargain. He displays the kind of courage he lacked while fighting in Spain and atones for his cowardice at that time.[1]

Huston coauthored the screenplay of *Key Largo* with Richard Brooks, who would follow Huston's lead and move up from being a scriptwriter to a writer and director of such movies as *The Blackboard Jungle* (1955). Huston and Brooks decamped to the Florida Keys to collaborate on the screenplay, since Huston was convinced that soaking up the atmosphere there would aid them in writing a more authentic script. They began by moving the setting of the story from 1939 to the post–World War II era. Moreover, they made Johnny Rocco a mob boss who sneaks back into the United States after he has been deported to Cuba by the U.S. government as an undesirable citizen. It was Brooks's suggestion that they model Rocco on Charles "Lucky" Luciano, a mobster deported to Cuba in 1946. Rocco, of course, was also based on Al Capone, who retired to Florida in the late 1940s and died there of advanced syphilis a year or so before the movie was made.[2]

Huston comments in his autobiography that, in bringing the play up to date, he and Brooks were depicting Rocco and his hoods as serving notice that the "underworld was on the move" in postwar America. Indeed, one of the gangsters in *Key Largo* predicts that when Rocco gets back on top, "it will be just like old times."

Edward G. Robinson thought that returning to Warner Bros. after a six-year absence to play Johnny Rocco, a heartless killer like Little Caesar, would give his career a boost. As a matter of fact, James Cagney would follow Robinson's lead and return to Warner a year later to make the gangster picture *White Heat* for the same reason.

Humphrey Bogart, who played in Huston's *The Treasure of Sierra Madre* (1948), plays Frank McCloud (King McCloud in the play), a World War II veteran who comes to Key Largo to pay a visit to the Largo Hotel. The proprietor is James Temple (Lionel Barrymore), who is confined to a wheelchair. James Temple is the father of George Temple, Mc-Cloud's deceased army buddy; Nora (Lauren Bacall) is George's widow. Claire Trevor, who played Bogart's old flame in *Dead End*, is Gaye Dawn, Rocco's erstwhile moll. Trevor remembers basing her portrayal of Gaye on "Luciano's mistress, Gay Orlova, an American showgirl [she] met in London in the early 1930s."[3]

The musical score is by Max Steiner (*White Heat*), and the cinematographer is Karl Freund, who worked with Fritz Lang in Berlin during the silent period. He won an Academy Award for *The Good Earth* (1937). Freund employed atmospheric shadows and bizarre lighting at times to transfigure the otherwise fairly commonplace hotel setting into a living nightmare. For example, Freund arranged the frightening setting, depicting a hurricane raging outside the hotel, with lights flickering and dimming, plus windows shattering and shutters banging.

Thomas Leitch praises *Key Largo* as "one of the great gangster films," and well he might. In *Little Caesar*, "Edward G. Robinson had almost single-handedly established the . . . gangster film genre."[4] In *Key Largo*, as Rocco, Robinson plays a ruthless gangster, like Rico in *Little Caesar*. Rocco plans a comeback as a gangland leader, aiming to terrorize law-abiding citizens, just as Rico had done during the Prohibition era.[5]

John McCarty reports that some critics found *Key Largo* "stagey" at times.[6] On the contrary, John Tibbetts compliments Huston, saying that, except for a few exterior scenes, Huston was wise to retain the "play's claustrophobic atmosphere by confining the action to the hotel interiors" because this helps to create tension.[7]

Like Wyler in *Dead End*, Huston primarily utilizes a single principal setting in filming a play. He rarely strays from the hotel setting throughout the film. Huston extends the action by staging scenes throughout the building, from the hotel lobby to the individual suites on the upper floors. The movement back and forth between the playing areas keeps the movie from being static or stagey. Finally, the shootout aboard the motor launch in the ocean at the film's end underscores the fact that Huston has made a cinematic film out of Anderson's play. Shooting lasted from December 1947 to March 1948.

Carlos Clarens says it is "rumored" that the showdown at sea was filmed by Raoul Walsh, but he gives no source for this information.[8] It is true, however, that Huston lifted the shootout for *Key Largo* from the final pages of Ernest Hemingway's novel *To Have and Have Not*, which Warner Bros. had filmed in 1944, without using the shootout in that film. Huston told *Time* magazine that he had "tried to make all the characters old-fashioned, to brand them as familiar figures from gangster films of the past," implying that they were ready to take over again. Certainly the racketeers in the film behave as if they were in a gangster film of the 1930s—not only Robinson, but Marc Lawrence, Thomas Gomez, and others.[9] Although Rocco's stay in the United States is temporary, he asserts more than once that he will be coming back when the time is right: "I'll be back on top one of these days!"

When *Key Largo* was submitted to the Breen Office, Stephen Jackson, Breen's chief consulter, wrote to producer Jerry Wald that he was concerned about Robinson's performance. Robinson was associated with the 1930s gangster cycle, which had caused a great deal of trouble for the censor's office. Wald replied that the film had a moral point to make, that is, that the gangster was the "symbol of everything we are trying to avoid going back to." Breen overruled Jackson's negative response to the film, since he sensed that Jackson was too inflexible in evaluating gangster films. Jackson, who was a judge before joining Breen's staff, was known as the "hanging judge" in the industry.[10]

The movie begins with a printed prologue: "At the southernmost point of the United States are the Florida Keys, a string of small islands held together by a concrete causeway. Largest of the remote coral islands is Key Largo." The first scene to follow the prologue shows Frank McCloud arriving on a bus at the old, isolated Hotel Largo to see George Temple's widow and father. Writes Huston, "I think *Key Largo* is best remembered by most people for the introductory scene with Eddie Robinson in the bathtub, cigar in mouth."[11] Scott Hammen adds, "By the time Robinson rises from the tub, still chomping on his cigar, and wraps himself in a silk bathrobe, his character has been completely defined for the moviegoer familiar with gangster pictures."[12]

Meanwhile, downstairs, McCloud relates some incidents about George Temple to James Temple and Nora, explaining how George died heroically in the Battle of San Pietro, a campaign about which Huston had made a documentary entitled *The Battle of San Pietro*. "The massive casualties, the ruined church, the improvised cemetery" are all in Huston's documentary.[13] McCloud admires George Temple and has nothing but contempt for Rocco, who attempts to provoke McCloud by handing him a gun and telling him to try and kill him. McCloud declines to have a gunfight with Rocco, so he tosses the gun on a chair, explaining that "one more Johnny Rocco in the world is not worth dying for." Rocco ridicules McCloud for being a coward: "A live war hero—now I know how you did it!" Then Deputy Sherriff Clyde Sawyer (John Rodney), whom Rocco is holding captive, impulsively grabs the gun and fires, but he is shot dead by Rocco. It seems that the gun Rocco gave to McCloud had no bullets in it. Gaye Dawn, running true to form as a dumb blonde, says, "A live coward is better than a dead hero." More to the point is Nora's comment to McCloud: "Maybe this is a rotten world, but a cause isn't lost as long as one person is willing to go on fighting." McCloud insists that he is *not* willing to fight Rocco's kind.

Rocco demands that Gaye, a lush, sing the old standby she used to warble as a nightclub singer in her heyday in exchange for a drink. Gaye struggles through "Moanin' Low," her voice flat and off-key. Revolted by her wretched performance, Rocco cruelly refuses her the drink. She is crushed and humiliated. Without a word, McCloud goes to the bar, pours a drink, and hands it to the grateful Gaye. Rocco is furious at being overruled and slaps McCloud around, but McCloud does not retaliate. McCloud's action demonstrates his innate courage, and his compassion for the woefully mistreated Gaye.

Rocco is a bully, but when a ferocious hurricane batters the hotel, he is terrified by the force of nature. Huston employs the hurricane to prefigure the violence that will erupt at the movie's climax. Meanwhile, another mob boss shows up with his entourage to purchase the counterfeit money Rocco has smuggled into the country. Ziggy (Marc Lawrence) buys the boodle of "funny money" and departs with his gang. Then Rocco demands that McCloud be skipper of the motor launch that will transport Rocco and his henchmen back to Cuba.

Rocco refuses to take Gaye along, and she surreptitiously lifts Rocco's gun from his pocket and slips it to McCloud. (Hell has no fury like a woman scorned.) En route to Cuba, McCloud summons the kind of courage he demonstrated in combat and confronts Rocco and his gang. The intrepid McCloud outmaneuvers and kills Rocco's gang, leaving Rocco hiding below deck. Rocco is waiting for his chance to take aim at McCloud, who is on deck, but McCloud shoots Rocco as he comes up the

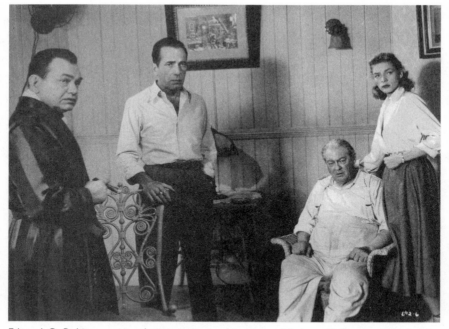

Edward G. Robinson again playing a gangster kingpin modeled on Al Capone (left) in John Huston's *Key Largo* (1948), with Humphrey Bogart (center) as his nemesis. Lionel Barrymore as James Temple and Lauren Bacall as Nora look on.

passageway, pretending to surrender. "The death of Johnny Rocco was intended to signify the end of an era," writes Barry Gifford; the days of the old-time gangster were over. "Organized crime moved into the modern world," and there was no place for the Johnny Roccos of yesteryear.[14]

Key Largo was a commercial success, although some reviewers merely thought it to be just another gangster flick. Jay Nash and Stanley Ross were right on target in calling it a "production against which most crime films can be judged and few can match."[15] Nevertheless, Huston decided that it was to be his last film for Warner Bros. Not only was he put off by Jack Warner's refusal to allow him to direct the projects he chose, he was "dissatisfied with the studio in general." Huston continued, "Its great innovative period was in decline," the days when Warner pioneered in the gangster genre, and the musical comedy genre, too.[16]

John Huston decided to become an independent filmmaker, making a deal with a studio for each film that he wanted to make, one picture at a time. While he was shopping around for his next property, Metro-Goldwyn-

Mayer (MGM) offered him *Quo Vadis*, but historical epics were not his cup of tea. He instead selected a project for which he was more suited and made a movie for MGM that turned out to be a major achievement.

The Asphalt Jungle (1950)

"The postwar crime cycle signaled the comeback of the gangster film," writes Jonathan Munby; "its return to popularity had been delayed by Hollywood's commitment to supporting the war effort" by making war pictures.[17] Huston contributed two gangster films to the renewal of the gangster genre. The first was *Key Largo*; then came *The Asphalt Jungle*, called the "granddaddy of the big heist films."[18] More recently, Dennis Lim has credited Huston with "creating the template of the heist film" by codifying its formula: "A criminal mastermind recruits a motley crew of outcasts with distinct personalities and functions"; the robbery sequence is precisely choreographed; and the "makeshift brotherhood dissolves, overtaken by paranoia and greed."[19]

The Asphalt Jungle was derived from a novel by W. R. Burnett, sometimes called the poet laureate of American crime fiction. Burnett also authored the novel on which *Little Caesar* is based, and he coauthored the screenplay for *This Gun for Hire*. As a screenwriter, Huston had already adapted Burnett's novel *High Sierra* for Humphrey Bogart in 1941. "Burnett almost seems to write for me," Huston once observed.[20]

Louis B. Mayer, the pompous vice president of MGM, was not pleased that Dore Schary, the production chief, had green-lighted *The Asphalt Jungle*. Mayer took one look at the script, coauthored by Huston and Ben Maddow, and snapped, saying, "It is full of nasty, ugly people, doing nasty, ugly things. I wouldn't walk across the room to see a thing like that."[21] But Nicholas Schenck, president of MGM's parent company, Loew's, sided with Schary, emphasizing to Mayer that MGM was still churning out too many bland movies, and not enough tough, gritty films like *The Asphalt Jungle*.[22] Schary furnished Huston with one of the studio's best cinematographers, Hal Rosson (*The Wizard of Oz*); together they turned out a "dark, claustrophobic film without a ray of sunshine filtering through" in most scenes.[23]

Ben Maddow, Huston's writing partner, agreed with him that a screenplay should be faithful to its literary source, which is certainly true of Huston's script for Dashiell Hammett's *The Maltese Falcon* (1941) and Maddow's script for William Faulkner's *Intruder in the Dust* (1949). There is little wonder that the screenplay for *The Asphalt Jungle* follows the novel so closely. What's more, Huston resisted making the changes to the screenplay suggested by Joseph Breen, the industry censor. Breen reminded Huston that the Motion Picture Production Code stated, "Methods of crime should not be explicitly presented: Theft, robbery, safecracking . . . should not be detailed in method," because such a detailed depiction of a crime might lead to its imitation in real life.[24] But the code was beginning to lose its bite in the 1950s. Hence, Huston was able to convince Breen to let this particular caveat pass.

Still, Breen had another complaint about the script to which he held tenaciously. During the course of the movie, Alonzo Emmerich, a crooked lawyer, commits suicide. Although suicide was not specifically forbidden by the code, Breen contended that suicide was prohibited by divine law and should be forbidden in motion pictures. When Emmerich kills himself in the screenplay, he does so calmly and deliberately, so Huston could not maintain that Emmerich was not in his right mind when he shot himself. Huston therefore altered the scene so that Emmerich hopelessly attempts to write a suicide note to his wife but is too agitated to complete it; he tears it up and discards it. The lawyer is thus shown to be in a state of turmoil at that moment and incapable of rational thought. That was sufficient to indicate, for the censor's purposes, that Emmerich "was not in his right mind" when he took his life.[25] Breen accepted the revised version of the scene and approved the screenplay. Furthermore, the code was amended the following year to include suicide among the actions discouraged.

Huston elicited a high degree of ensemble acting from a group of supporting players who rarely got the opportunity to give performances of such substance. Sam Jaffe took the role as Doc Riedenschneider, a German American and the mastermind of the armed robbery; Louis Calhern is the corrupt lawyer Alonzo Emmerich; Marc Lawrence, who played a mob boss in *Key Largo*, is Cobby, a bookie who has connections with the mob; Jean Hagen is Doll, a former dancer in a clip joint and Dix Handley's melancholy mistress; and Sterling Hayden is the brooding loser Dix. Huston had trouble selling Hayden to Schary because Hayden was an irritable loner in real life; his resume also included some mediocre movies, as he had been in more turkeys than Stove Top dressing. Withal, he gives a commanding performance in *The Asphalt Jungle*. Dix grew up on a Kentucky horse farm, on which the banks have foreclosed, and he earnestly yearns to go home again before he dies. The only actress in the cast lacking experience was a young Marilyn Monroe, who made her first notable movie appearance in this picture as Emmerich's feather-brained mistress Angela.

Huston shot the movie in just forty-nine days and was quite satisfied with it when it was finished. He made a short promo for the film, in which he addresses the audience, saying that the movie is about a little band of criminals and their relationships with one another. "You may not admire these people, but I think they'll fascinate you," he says.

In postwar gangster pictures, the city has become more dark and disturbing than ever before. Huston portrays the city (which goes unnamed, but is probably Chicago) as a grimy, hostile wilderness, little different from a jungle. Although the city in the film is identified as being in the Midwest, the movie was filmed in Los Angeles.

The key players in John Huston's *The Asphalt Jungle* (1950); bottom row, left to right: Sam Jaffe, Louis Calhern, Jean Hagen, and Sterling Hayden.

The movie begins with a gray dawn that casts light on a "wasteland of train tracks, desolate-looking warehouses, dingy oil storage tanks, and grimy alleys full of rubble."[26] Then Rosson's camera picks up a thug prowling down deserted streets, hiding behind a pillar next to a train track from a passing patrol car; it is Dix Handley.

We soon cut to Doc Riedenschneider, recently released from prison, emerging from a taxi and entering a shady bookie joint. He goes down a long dark corridor to meet with Cobby, the bookmaker, in his grubby office. Doc arranges through Cobby to have an audience with the patrician lawyer Emmerich. Doc confers with Emmerich, not in his house in town, but in his riverside cottage, where he keeps his nubile mistress, Angela. He agrees to underwrite the expenses of setting up the heist in return for the right to fence the diamonds Doc intends to steal from Belletier's Jewelry store. Doc describes the heist as the "biggest caper ever to be pulled in the Midwest." He explains that three key members of the gang will be paid a flat fee up front for their services, "like house painters": the safe cracker, Louis Ciavelli (Anthony Caruso); the getaway driver, Gus Minissi (Jamew Whitmore); and the gunman, Dix Handley.

Emmerich is in cahoots with a private eye named Brannom (not Brannon, as some critics spell it). He informs Brannom that he is broke and intends to keep the diamonds for himself to finance his high living for the rest of his life. He plans on leaving for parts unknown with the loot as soon as possible, thereby double-crossing Doc and the rest of the gang.

Huston portrays the actual diamond heist in eleven minutes of nearly wordless screen time. The movie's "meticulous and spellbinding robbery sequence set the standard for every heist film to come in the gangster genre."[27] When Louis blows the safe with nitroglycerin, he inadvertently triggers a hidden burglar alarm, and police sirens can be heard almost immediately coming toward the jewelry store. But the gang finishes collecting the jewels from the safe before leaving. Louis is fatally wounded in a scuffle with a security guard, and the thieves retreat from the scene by crawling through a sewer.

Doc and Dix head for Emmerich's baronial mansion in town, where Emmerich confronts them in the company of Brannom. In his sitting room, Emmerich informs Doc and Dix that he is broke and could not raise the funds to defray the expenses of the caper as he had hoped. A shootout ensues between Dix and Brannom, in which Brannom is killed and Dix is seriously injured. Dix and Doc depart, planning to meet with Emmerich after he promises they can soon settle their accounts. Meanwhile, Doc holds on to the jewels. Emmerich plays cards with his bedridden wife. She ruefully admits that she is scared of the criminal types that he associates with. In the best-remembered line of dialogue from the film, Emmerich responds to his wife, "There's nothing so different about them; crime is only a left-handed form of human endeavor."

One by one, Doc's partners in crime are tracked down by the police and cajoled into confessing their part in the robbery. Two policemen arrive at Emmerich's mansion in town and tell him that they have reason to believe that he is involved with the gang that committed the robbery. His answers to their questions are evasive. After they leave, he flees to his cottage on the river, but the police follow him there and arrest him. He asks them to permit him to write a letter to his wife, and he retires to the next room to do so. In despair, he cannot bring himself to complete the letter and destroys it. He then takes his gun from a drawer and shoots himself, unable to face disgrace and ruin.

When he hears of the suicide of Emmerich, the death of Louis, and other misfortunes, Doc reflects that these mishaps that have followed in the wake of the robbery are the results of blind accident: "What can you do about blind accidents?" As Steve says in *Criss Cross*, "It's Fate; it's in the cards." It is part of the German ethos that Fate influences people's lives. Doc speaks of the intervention of blind accident in one's life; putting it another way, he speaks elsewhere in the movie of one being influenced by one's vices. He is saying that flawed human beings must sooner or later reckon with their flawed characters. This will be apparent in Doc's fate by film's end.

As the police close in, Doc hires a taxi to drive him to another big town, out of the reach of the local cops. He stops in a diner for some supper and immediately becomes smitten with a young teenage girl who is gyrating to the music of a juke box. She is not particularly alluring and is dressed in a rather plain outfit. Thus, Huston is implying that Doc's interest in this nymphet is purely sexual. As Doc says early in the film, "We all work for our vices." Doc's vice is tender-aged girls, just as Emmerich's vice is extravagance, as Huston notes in the promo for the film, mentioned earlier. Doc does not notice that two policemen are observing him through the window of the diner. When he leaves the establishment, they frisk him and find the jewels, which are sewn in the lining of his coat. If he had not lingered to watch the nymphet, he could have gotten away before the police noticed him. Fate, he believes, has allowed blind accident to assert itself in his life while he was preoccupied with the nymphet.

The most compelling scene in the picture is the last one, when Dix, mortally wounded, endeavors to return to his roots by driving to Hickory Wood Farm in Kentucky, with Doll by his side. Weakened by his loss of blood, he staggers into a bluegrass field on the farm and breathes his last breath. "In the film's final shot, he lies dead in a wide Kentucky meadow, while three horses graze around him, nuzzling his body."[28] Dix had hoped to escape the corrosive atmosphere of the asphalt jungle by his flight with Doll to a cleaner rural environment, but for Dix, brutalized by a life of crime, it is already too late.

Munby believes that *The Asphalt Jungle* is one of Huston's finest achievements. The film's "action takes place in a nameless urban environment," although one can recognize the cityscape of Los Angeles, highlighted by the City Hall Tower in the opening credits, with the city's "suburban sprawl." The gang put together by the German criminal genius Doc Riedenschneider is "comprised of various social misfits," including an Italian American safe cracker "with mouths to feed and rent to pay," and a seedy bookmaker. "The gang constitutes a false community brought together in the common interest of committing a crime," a gang that will inevitably disintegrate when things go wrong.[29]

W. R. Burnett applauded the movie as "without a doubt one of the best films of this genre."[30] John Huston pointed out that Sam Jaffe won the best actor award at the Venice Film Festival as the "good doctor who has the brains of the gang" but could not tear himself away from the sight of a young girl shaking her backside, "thereby causing his own downfall."[31] This brings into relief how Huston took pains to give the characters a human dimension. After all, Huston explains, "Unless you understand the criminal, there is no way of coping with him."[32]

THE LADY FROM SHANGHAI
AND THE GREAT GATSBY

The Lady from Shanghai (1947)

Orson Welles liked to tell the story of how he came to make *The Lady from Shanghai*. He said that in 1946, he was on tour with a stage production of *Around the World in Eighty Days* when Michael Todd, the producer, went broke in Boston. On a hunch, Welles phoned Harry Cohn, the head of Columbia Pictures in Hollywood, telling Cohn that if he would wire him the money to keep his show on the road, he would make a film adaptation of a novel for Columbia. "I'll write it, direct it, and star in it," he said.[1] When Cohn asked him for the title of the novel he wanted to film, Welles looked at the paperback display next to the pay phone he was using and spied a novel entitled *If I Die Before I Wake*, by Sherwood King. He gave that title to Cohn. Cohn said that he would send Welles the money he needed, and in return he expected Welles to direct the movie for free, although he would be paid for acting in it and directing it. Consequently, Welles committed himself to filming a book he had not even read—a nice anecdote, but apocryphal.

For a start, King's novel was not available in paperback in 1946. Moreover, Columbia already owned the screen rights to the novel, so Cohn did not have to purchase them for Welles, as Welles had assumed. Cohn commissioned Welles to make the movie, displacing the original director, William Castle.[2] Cohn wanted Rita Hayworth, the reigning star at Columbia, to play the lead. Although Hayworth was Welles's estranged wife, they both agreed to do the picture. (They divorced when the picture was finished.)

The Lady from Shanghai is often considered a film noir, but, like *Criss Cross*, it also bears the marks of a gangster film—Hayworth's character is connected to a Chinatown gang. As Tom Conley writes, "*The Lady from Shanghai* cannot be easily classified."[3] Neither can *Criss Cross* (see chapter 5).

Michael O'Hara (Orson Welles), an Irish sailor, is victimized by the "machinations wrought by Elsa Bannister (Rita Hayworth), in collusion with her husband, Arthur (Everett Sloane), an aging cane-swaggering cripple who happens to be a brilliant criminal lawyer," and, by his own admission, a canny criminal, like Alonzo Emmerich in *The Asphalt Jungle*.[4] Arthur, together with his slippery law partner, George Grisby (Glenn Anders), swindles their clients, in league with Elsa, who has a gang in Chinatown she can call upon when she is in need, as already mentioned.

Harry Cohn, who once said that movies are not a business, but a racket, was a demanding boss. He did not hesitate to have Welles's production office bugged so he could monitor Welles's daily progress on the film. Every day, when Welles reported for work, he would announce, "Welcome to another day of fascinating good listening."[5] Welles used the "super market" approach to adapting a novel into a screenplay, picking what he wanted from King's novel and bypassing the rest. He also added elements of his own. On the one hand, his Elsa is much the same character that Sherwood King created. On the other hand, the unusual shootout in the "Magic Mirror Maze," which climaxes the film, is not in the novel at all. Welles's shooting script is dated September 20, 1946.

Prior to the beginning of principal photography, Welles had Rita Hayworth shorn of her long red tresses and her short hair dyed platinum blond. After all, she could not look like the pinup she had been for American gigs during World War II. Welles explained, "She was going to play the kind of person she'd never been on the screen," a real villainess.[6] "Elsa is the duplicitous and deadly female, . . . all the more dangerous because of her beauty and deceptive nature."[7] She is a femme fatale like Anna in *Criss Cross*.

Principal photography commenced in November 1946, in Acapulco, with Errol Flynn's yacht standing in for the Bannister's yacht, and Flynn as skipper. When Welles and the production unit returned to Hollywood in January 1947, Welles worked with special effects wizard Lawrence Butler (*The Thief of Bagdad*) to create the Magic Mirror Maze for the last sequence. Cinematographer Charles Lawton Jr. (*The Black Arrow*) was Columbia's first-rank director of photography. Welles had Columbia's best craftsmen working for him. He and Lawton agreed to employ natural lighting for exteriors to give the film the realistic look of a newsreel, which was quite suitable for a gangster film.[8]

Filming lasted ninety-eight days, ending on January 27, 1947. When Welles showed his rough cut of 155 minutes to Cohn and his minions, the studio chieftain was appalled. He offered $1,000 to anyone who could explain the story to him.[9] Cohn assigned his chief editor, Viola Lawrence (*Cover Girl*) to shorten the film and clarify the plot. She came up with an eighty-six-minute version that was not received well when the studio held a couple of sneak previews—not surprisingly, since removing more than an hour of footage, some of it necessary exposition, did real harm to the narrative continuity of the story line. The film was presumably shortened so drastically so that it could play on a double bill, like a low-budget movie. At any rate, Michael's narration, which was not in the shooting script, was added at Cohn's behest to fill in the gaps in the narrative.[10] The picture was given a limited release, mostly in neighborhood theaters, and flopped. It cost $2 million to make and took in $1.5 million.[11] The profit-minded Cohn never hired Welles again; Welles made only one more movie in Hollywood and then decamped for Europe. It was a decade before he made another Hollywood movie.

The Lady from Shanghai starts out with a night scene in Central Park, in which Elsa is riding in a horse-drawn carriage. A gang of underworld hoodlums pounces on her and drags her into the bushes, but she is rescued by Michael O'Hara. He comments, voice-over on the sound track, that he is "very far from being the hero that his easy victory might make him seem."[12] We later learn that the scuffle in the park was a setup, engineered by Elsa to make it possible for her to meet Michael, so she could embroil him in her scheme to rid herself of Arthur. She, in fact, hired the gang of thugs that pretended to be kidnapping her.

As they ride in her hackney cab, Elsa sketches her background for him. She explains that she was born of white Russian parents in Chifu, and has worked in the "wickedest cities in the world," including Shanghai. She implies that she was implicated in a vice ring in Shanghai, but the Motion Picture Production Code barred a character from giving specific details about prostitution, "which should never be more than suggested, and only when essential to the plot."[13] She also confesses that she worked in a gambling casino, but adds ruefully, "You need more than luck in Shanghai." Because Asians were stereotyped at the time as sinister and inscrutable, the fact that Elsa grew up in China gives her an alien, inscrutable quality to an American audience, like Mother Gin Sling in Josef von Sternberg's *The Shanghai Gesture* (1941). In sum, Elsa had a nasty, sordid record in China, which is why she fled to the United States.

Elsa later asks Arthur to engage Michael as a crew member for their cruise to San Francisco by way of Acapulco. Arthur walks with two canes, one for each of his crippled legs. He is twisted physically, which suggests that he is also twisted psychologically, for he is an evil and corrupt lawyer. Harry Cohn demanded that Rita Hayworth sing a torch song in the picture, because she had made some successful musicals for Columbia, like *Cover Girl*. The hypnotic siren song, which she sings aboard the yacht, serves the purposes of the plot by helping to lure Michael to fall for her. The yacht is appropriately named the *Circe*, a bewitching enchantress in classical lore who transformed heroes into swine.

The yacht stops for a picnic on a Mexican island; when night falls, the picnic on the beach is lit by glowing torches, a fine example of Welles's use of source lighting in the film. The picnic is a chiaroscuro of torchlight against dark water, an appropriate atmosphere for the Bannisters to discuss their dark pasts. Arthur tells Michael that even though Elsa was involved in some sordid situations in Shanghai, his past legal transactions would shock Michael.

Michael then recalls that in Brazil, he once witnessed an injured shark bleeding in the water; the scent of blood drove the other sharks mad, and they fed on one another. In their frenzy, they even ate at themselves. He concludes, "I never saw anything worse than that—until this little picnic tonight." Heylin comments astutely that, "Michael is adrift in a sea of sharks,"[14] but Michael accurately describes in his shark tale the self-destructive inclinations of the Bannisters, which will become painfully apparent by film's end.

Michael is infatuated with Elsa but lacks the funds to take her away from Arthur; therefore, he readily "listens to Grisby's almost farcical proposition about feigning Grisby's murder, so that he may go off to the South Seas" to escape his shrewish wife and an impending nuclear holocaust. (The film takes place only a few years after the United States dropped atomic bombs on Japan.) Grisby's story is filled with discrepancies; for example, he has no wife.[15] Nevertheless, Michael even signs a bogus document that states that he accidentally shot Grisby to death.

After the *Circe* docks in San Francisco, Michael and Elsa have a clandestine meeting at the San Francisco Aquarium to discuss her prospects of escaping Arthur's clutches. Welles photographed Michael and Elsa separately from his filming of the monstrous fish in the tanks. That way he could splice a shot of the appropriate fish swimming into view that would fit with what the pair were talking about at that moment. Thus, Elsa's mentioning of her brutal husband coincides with a shot of a shark swimming by.

Sidney Broome (Ted de Corsia), a private detective disguised as the Bannister's butler, attempts to blackmail Grisby by informing him that he has learned of his plot to murder Arthur Bannister so that Elsa will run away with him, and frame Michael for the crime. Grisby, chagrined and caught off guard, shoots Broome dead. Grisby himself then turns up dead; Michael is accused of killing him because the police have discovered the written agreement Michael made with Grisby to murder him. The police cannot find the gun that killed Grisby, and Arthur, who is defending Michael in court, admits that he cannot prove that Michael is innocent without it.

While waiting for the verdict at his trial, Michael swallows Arthur's pain pills to make his guards think that he is attempting suicide; he then escapes from the courthouse and flees to Chinatown. As he runs away from the courthouse, Welles's camera records him as a tiny figure diminishing into the distance. Michael, we realize, is a small man lost in a large and complex world. Elsa follows Michael to Chinatown.

Raymond Borde and Etienne Chaumeton write that it is "regrettable that certain scenes relating to the relation between Miss Bannister and the Chinese community have been cut."[16] Nevertheless, in the Chinatown sequence, there is evidence that Elsa speaks Cantonese fluently and is familiar with many inhabitants of Chinatown, who address her as "Xinlin Zhang." Elsa's contacts help her to catch up with Michael in a Chinese playhouse called the Mandarin Theater. She goes backstage and phones Lee (Li) Gong, a Chinatown gang leader who masquerades as the Bannister's chauffeur, at his mob's hangout. It is clear that Lee and his racketeers have helped Elsa in the past with her skullduggery.

Elsa says to her underworld crony in Cantonese, "Please help me." Lee, the mob boss, replies in Cantonese, "You give me a hard time; why should I help you?" We cut to Lee and his cohorts piling into a car, on the way to the Mandarin Theater.[17]

Elsa finds Michael hiding among the audience at the play and sits next to him. While conferring with Elsa, he discovers a gun in her purse and guesses quite rightly that it is the weapon that was used to murder Grisby; Michael then passes out from the pain pills he swallowed. Lee and his gang appear in the auditorium and, on Elsa's orders, kidnap Michael. They take him to a deserted amusement park that is closed for the season.

When he awakens, Michael wanders through the park's Fun House and tumbles down a slippery slide, right through the jaws of a papier-mâché dragon. He ends up in the murky Hall of Mirrors, also known as the Magic Mirror Maze. There he encounters Elsa, who is holding a gun; she shines a flashlight on him while she sheds light on her scheme. Grisby, she explains, "lost his silly head" and shot Broome when Broome attempted to blackmail him. Aware that Grisby was becoming erratic, and therefore unpredictable, she shot him. She then arranged a kangaroo trial, in which Arthur would serve as Michael's defense lawyer and see to it that Michael took the fall for Grisby's death.

Suddenly Arthur appears, brandishing a gun and saying, "I knew I would find you two together." He quite wrongly assumes that Elsa has decided to go away with Michael. "Are you aiming at me, lover? Because I'm aiming at you," he says. Arthur continues: "Of course, killing you is like killing myself, but, you know, I'm pretty tired of both of us." The mirror images of Arthur and Elsa are "multiplied prismatically, as they seek to shoot their images to bits," Conley writes. Mayhem ensues, with "bullets shattering mirrors, until they reach the two spouses."[18] Michael comments in his voice-over that they are "like the sharks, chewing away at each other."

Elsa had hoped to get rid of both Arthur and Grisby—and Michael, too, so that she could be free to spend the Bannister fortune on herself. Instead she lies dying on the floor of the Magic Mirror Maze, amid the blood and broken glass. She futilely calls out to Michael as he goes through the exit. Then she murmurs, "Give my love to the sunrise," for she realizes that she will never see another one.

Orson Welles and Rita Hayworth in Welles's movie *The Lady from Shanghai* (1947).

The camera rises above the boardwalk of the amusement park as Michael walks toward the dawn of a new day. He muses on the sound track, "Maybe I'll live so long that I'll forget her; maybe I'll die trying."

The movie was a box-office failure in the United States. Peter Bogdanovich cites Welles in his DVD commentary as saying, "The first indication I had that it was a good picture was when I got to Europe after it had opened in the United States."[19] It was very well received, particularly in France, where it was hailed as one of Welles's major works. Furthermore, the reputation of the film has steadily grown throughout the years. *Time*'s obituary for Welles singles out the "hall-of-mirrors gunfight in *The Lady from Shanghai*" as a scene that is unforgettable.[20] As David Thomson puts it, the movie has "some of the greatest things Welles would ever do, things so black that they should never be forgotten or explained away."[21] A lady gangster who was involved with a vice ring in China and a Chinese mob in San Francisco, as well as with her lawyer-husband's schemes, makes quite a leading lady for a gangster picture.

The Great Gatsby (1949)

About the time that Orson Welles was going to Europe to continue his filmmaking career, Paramount was looking for a strong role for Alan Ladd to play in his next picture. They offered him the title role in *The Great Gatsby*, adapted from F. Scott Fitzgerald's 1925 novel. As it happened, when Scott and Zelda Fitzgerald moved to Great Neck, Long Island, in 1922, their neighbors were some well-to-do bootleggers. The hero of Fitzgerald's novel is Jay Gatsby, whose shady activities as a racketeer were modeled on the criminal behavior of the gangsters who surrounded the Fitzgeralds on Long Island.

The key source for Gatsby was Max Gerlach, who lived near the Fitzgeralds in Great Neck. The closest link between Gerlach the bootlegger and Gatsby is a note that Gerlach sent to Fitzgerald on July 20, 1923, which reads, "How are you and the family, old sport?"[22] The last two words reflect Gatsby's way of greeting his friends, which mirrors the studied nonchalance of someone trying too hard to make a good impression on others.

One of Gatsby's disreputable associates, Meyer Wolfsheim, was also drawn from life. He was based on Arnold Rothstein, a vice lord and bootlegger whom Fitzgerald once met. He was responsible for having fixed the 1919 World Series. When Gatsby introduces Nick Carraway to Wolfsheim in the novel, Nick is astonished to learn that the latter single-handedly engineered the Black Sox Scandal. It had never occurred to Nick that one man could tamper with the faith of millions of people with the "single-mindedness of a burglar blowing a safe." In this passage, then, Fitzgerald lets the reader know the kind of company that Gatsby, whose real name is Gatz, keeps.

Early in the novel, Gatsby has moved into an estate in West Egg, Long Island, where he meets the book's narrator, Nick Carraway, his neighbor. He earnestly requests that Nick introduce him to Daisy Buchanan, who lives with her husband Tom in the more fashionable East Egg, across the bay. Gatsby and Daisy were actually lovers during World War I, when Gatsby was in the army, in the days before Daisy married stockbroker Tom Buchanan. Since then, Gatsby has cheapened himself in his efforts to get rich quick so that he can woo Daisy away from Tom.

Screenwriter DeWitt Bodeen coaxed Alan Ladd into reading Fitzgerald's novel, and Ladd became anxious to do the movie.[23] Hence, Paramount decided to make a sound version of *The Great Gatsby*, which the studio had made as a silent picture (now lost) in 1926. Not all of the versions of *The Great Gatsby* done for film emphasize that Gatsby was a real gangster and not just a shady businessman. The 1974 movie, for example, only suggests that Gatsby is a mobster by having Nick note that Gatsby's "butler" is really his bodyguard and carries a gun at all times. But the 1949 film makes no bone about Gatsby's status as a criminal, as we shall see.

The producer and co-screenwriter was Richard Maibaum, who later scripted several James Bond pictures, starting with *Dr. No*; Cyril Hume was co-screenwriter. Orson Welles once said, "There is nothing more cinematic than narration, because . . . anything that helps you see more clearly is cinematic, and narration can help you see more clearly."[24] Consequently, Nick Carraway narrates the movie, just as he narrates the novel.

Elliott Nugent, the director, worried that he had bitten off more than he could chew when he took on *The Great Gatsby*. Nugent may have drawn some reassurance from the fact that the cinematographer, John Seitz (*This Gun for Hire*), was collaborating with him; Seitz was widely known as the best black-and-white director of photography in Hollywood. The Maibaum–Hume script was a fine piece of work. The screenwriters consulted Owen Davis's 1926 Broadway version of the novel, which adhered closely to the book in composing the screen adaptation.

The final shooting script includes a prologue that takes place at Gatsby's burial, where Nick (Macdonald Carey) chats with Jordan Baker (Ruth Hussey), Nick's erstwhile girlfriend. The date on Gatsby's tombstone is 1928. Nick and Jordan are among the few mourners present because the word on the street is that Gatsby's death was presumably a gangland killing.

Nick begins his expository narration by describing the Jazz Age, speaking of "careless dancing, rum runners, and gang wars." Irene Atkins, whose essay on *The Great Gatsby* films is excellent, notes that Nick's remarks are accompanied by "stock shots from old gangster films."[25] In addition, shots of Alan Ladd, clearly visible as he shoots a submachine gun, are interpolated into the stock footage. Gatsby's criminal connections are stressed more in the 1949 film than in the novel or the other film versions of the book. This was done to capitalize on the "tough guy" image Ladd had established with the mass audience in such films as *This Gun for Hire* (see chapter 4).

Later in the movie Reba (Jack Lambert), a gangster with whom Gatsby has had some dealings, shows up at one of Gatsby's posh week-end parties. The surly thug embarrasses Gatsby by drunkenly insisting on discussing "business" and insolently addressing him repeatedly as Gatz (his real surname). Gatsby graciously invites the intruder to join him behind a high hedge in the garden, where he summarily knocks the intruder cold and then discreetly instructs the butler to hustle the of-fending guest off the property. Although the incident is not in the novel, it is decidedly in keeping with the spirit of the book, since it exempli-fies Gatsby's concerted effort to keep the tainted nature of his gangster activities a secret from Daisy (Betty Field) by dissociating himself from the likes of Reba in public.

This version of *The Great Gatsby* was directed by Elliott Nugent *(The Male Animal)*, a conscientious craftsman whose films nonetheless seldom turned out to be of more than routine interest. When Nugent directed *The Great Gatsby*, he was beset with emotional problems. Subject to clinical depression, he was afraid that he would not do justice to the book, which he considered to be "Scott Fitzgerald's best novel and perhaps the best of all American novels." As the time for shooting approached, he recalls in his autobiography that he had serious misgivings about his ability to make a worthy motion picture of *Gatsby*. He even considered committing suicide. Just before shooting started, he writes, "my mood had changed, and I was scoffing at my foolish terror."[26]

Richard Maibaum, co-scriptwriter and producer of the film, sensed Ladd's kinship with the role of Gatsby one evening when he was visiting Ladd at home. The star showed him his expensive wardrobe, including row after row of elegant shirts, thereby recalling Gatsby proudly displaying his wardrobe, particularly his collection of fancy shirts, to Daisy the first time she comes to his mansion. "Not bad for an Okie kid, eh?" Gatsby says. Maibaum remembers Ladd saying to him, "My God!" Maibaum thought to himself, *He's Gatsby!*[27] In brief, Fitzgerald described Gatsby as an elegant young roughneck, and Ladd filled that role perfectly.

Howard Da Silva played George Wilson, the husband of Myrtle Wil-son, Tom Buchanan's mistress, in the 1949 *Gatsby*, and Meyer Wolfsheim in the 1974 remake, starring Robert Redford. He believed that Ladd's han-dling of the part was superior to Redford's. "As much as I admired Redford as an actor, I felt that he never could play a man from the opposite side of

Alan Ladd in the title role of *The Great Gatsby* (1949), based on the novel by F. Scott Fitzgerald. Betty Field plays Daisy Buchanan.

the tracks," Da Silva explained. "Ladd could and did."[28] Furthermore, although some critics judged that Betty Field (*Of Mice and Men*) came across as petulant in the role of the haughty Daisy, she "captured the demeanor of the person, and the emotion, behind that demeanor."[29]

Some explanation of Gatsby's past, particularly his youthful association with his mentor, Dan Cody (Henry Hull), is important to the understanding of Gatsby's character. As a matter of fact, the movie is faithful to its source in its attempt to gradually sketch Gatsby's background for the viewer with the aid of flashbacks. In one flashback, Gatsby recounts for Nick how a self-made millionaire named Dan Cody took him under his wing when he was still a youngster, allowing him to serve as a mate on the old man's yacht. It was under Cody's tutelage that this teenage lad confirmed his resolution to discard his former identity as James Gatz to forge a new personality for himself as Jay Gatsby.

Dan Cody, a rambunctious old sourdough whom Fitzgerald named after Daniel Boone and "Buffalo Bill" Cody, made his fortune in the Wild West. Hence, the advice that this tough old buzzard passes on to his foster son has a ruthless, materialistic ring to it, based as it is on the assumption that one's personal happiness is derived almost exclusively on the size of his bankroll. Cody was a racketeer who is still referred to as an "old devil." So in the film, when former serviceman Jay Gatsby, who courted Daisy while he was in the armed forces, learns that he has lost Daisy to millionaire Tom Buchanan, the camera zooms in on a photograph of Cody on his bureau as Jay murmurs, "The old gentleman was right; you can't compete without money."

Some of the symbolic nuances of the novel, for instance, the green light that burns each night at the end of the pier fronting the Buchanan mansion, were incorporated into the film's script. Nick Carraway first notices the green light glowing on Daisy's dock when he spies Gatsby gazing at it as he stands on his own front lawn, stretching his arms toward the dark water that separates East Egg from West Egg, and thus separates him from Daisy. The color green, because of its association with the renewal of nature in the springtime, implies Gatsby's hope that he will eventually be able to traverse the distance that divides Daisy's world from his and possess her once more.[30]

Another effective visual image incorporated into the film from the book is that of the Valley of Ashes, which lies between New York and Long Island. Sara Mayfield notes that whenever Fitzgerald traveled on a commuter train from Great Neck to the city, he noticed the "wastelands along the tracks."[31] He decided that the desolate area, marred by mounds of ashes and refuse, would be the proper place to locate Wilson's garage and the shabby flat he shares with Myrtle (Shelley Winters). This highlights the contrast between the dismal environment in which the Wilsons live and the lush landscape surrounding the estates of the Buchanans and their aristocratic coterie. The misguided Gatsby fails to understand that Daisy is willing to carry on a furtive affair with him, but at no time would she seriously consider leaving her husband for a social-climbing gangster, a gate crasher in her privileged world.

Near Wilson's garage in the Valley of Ashes, in the film as in the book, there is a billboard advertising an oculist by the name of Dr. T. J. Eckleburg, which depicts a pair of enormous eyes rimmed in spectacles, surveying the depressing dumping ground that stretches in front of the sign. For Fitzgerald, the eyes had a far-reaching significance. "The great, unblinking eyes, expressionless, looking down upon the human scene," as Maxwell Perkins, Fitzgerald's literary editor at Scribner's, later described them, symbolized for Fitzgerald "nothing less than the eyes of God Himself."[32] This symbolic meaning of the eyes on the poster, which would be carried over from the novel to the film, is emphasized in the scene in which Wilson, while charging his wife with adultery, points to the eyes staring down at her from the signboard across the way and solemnly reminds her that God sees everything: "You may fool me, but you can't fool God."[33]

The religious implications of the oculist's billboard are underscored in the movie when Gatsby stops at Wilson's garage with a sidekick from his army days, Klipspringer (Elisha Cook Jr.), en route to his home in West Egg. Noticing the oculist's poster, Klipspringer says with a touch of awe in his voice, "Those eyes getcha—like God bought himself a pair of eyeglasses, so He could watch us better."

Klipspringer's remark is visualized several times on the screen throughout the course of the movie. The eyes on the billboard are visible as they seemingly "watch" Tom (Barry Sullivan) surreptitiously picking up Myrtle down the road a bit from the gas station for one of their trysts, as well as in the sequence in which Tom finds the battered body of Myrtle, the victim of a hit-and-run driver, lying near the Eckleburg sign.

The oculist's signboard, which is the last image to appear on the screen at the film's final fadeout, is used so effectively throughout the film to remind the viewer of Klipspringer's thought-provoking remark that cinema critic Manny Farber must have been only half-joking when he quipped in his notice for the movie that the "oculist's billboard, with the enormous spectacled eyes, steals the movie."[34]

What Daisy does not know about Gatsby—but that her husband makes it his business to find out—is that most of Gatsby's fortune is derived from a number of unsavory criminal operations, of which bootlegging is only a part. Gatsby, in short, is a racketeer who is involved with various New York gangsters, like Meyer Wolfsheim. Tom reveals the facts about Gatsby while they are on a foray to New York one summer afternoon. Daisy is overwhelmed by Tom's revelations; while driving back to Long Island from New York City, she accidentally runs over Tom's mistress, Myrtle, right in front of Wilson's gas station. Both Tom and Daisy allow Gatsby to personally assume the blame for the hit-and-run killing because Tom wants to exonerate his beloved Daisy of any guilt.

The coincidence that seems inherent in Tom's wife being behind the wheel of the car that runs down his mistress was criticized by some critics as too facile and contrived. On the contrary, the screenwriters make it quite clear that Myrtle dashes out onto the highway to try and stop the car speeding past her husband's gas station because she assumes that it is Tom—and not Daisy—who is driving the automobile. She attempts to flag down the speeding vehicle because she wants Tom to protect her from the wrath of her husband George, who has discovered that she is having an affair with Buchanan. The screenwriters have created a moment of sheer terror with the ill-fated death car, the "frantic expression of Myrtle Wilson, the ugly sound of fender against flesh."[35] Accordingly, the screenwriters have orchestrated this catastrophe with far more plausibility than they have usually been given credit for.

As a result of his taking the rap for Myrtle's death, Gatsby is shot to death by Myrtle's revenge-crazed husband, George. He shoots the man he believes is responsible for his wife's death. Jay Gatsby, he is convinced, robbed him of the one thing of value he possessed in his otherwise miserable existence. Why should we assume that Myrtle meant any less to George than Daisy meant to Gatsby? Hence, after killing Gatsby, George turns the gun on himself and commits suicide.

The 1949 version of *The Great Gatsby* ends with Nick Carraway and Jordan Baker at Gatsby's graveside; after bidding good-bye to Jay (née James Gatz), the two realize that they are in love and decide to marry. By contrast, the novel ends with Nick going back to the Midwest, where he came from, without Jordan. American films at the time still tended to have happy endings because the studios feared that audiences would reject downbeat conclusions. Consequently, Paramount's front office thought it wise that Nick and Jordan get together at the end, although the novel has no such upbeat ending.

As for Gatsby, one of the mourners at his sparsely attended funeral delivers a benediction for him that appears at the end of the book: "The poor son-of-bitch." This phrase was repeated by fiction writer and screenwriter Dorothy Parker at Fitzgerald's wake, which attracted few mourners in Hollywood, where he finished his career as a failed screenwriter in 1940.[36]

It is easy to agree with the critics who see the 1949 edition of *The Great Gatsby* as a serious attempt to do justice to Fitzgerald's masterpiece, without sweeping under the rug the fact that Gatsby was a gangster.

"Somehow," Nugent concludes, "we got the picture finished. While it never completely satisfied me, it received good reviews and was a financial success."[37] Without question, the 1949 *Gatsby* was the most distinguished picture Nugent ever turned out, and Ladd's portrayal of Gatsby has come to be considered, along with his role as Raven in *This Gun for Hire*, one of his best performances of his career, what some have called an example of perfect casting.

The fifth motion-picture version of *The Great Gatsby* premiered in 2013. For the record, the Australian director Baz Luhrmann (*Moulin Rouge!*) selected Leonardo DiCaprio for the title role, which is something less than perfect casting. Like Robert Redford in the 1974 *Gatsby*, DiCaprio is a bit too slick and sleek to be Fitzgerald's Gatsby. Since the 1974 and 2013 movies, which are in color, have overshadowed the 1949 Ladd version, I have given it a reassessment here. What's more, the Ladd film is essentially a gangster picture, with Gatsby portrayed as a "surly, social-climbing bootlegger."[38] Hence it belongs in this book.

FRITZ LANG'S *YOU ONLY LIVE ONCE* AND *THE BIG HEAT*

You Only Live Once (1937)

Vienna-born Fritz Lang was working in the film industry in Berlin when Hitler came to power. He fled to Hollywood in 1934, where he made his first American movie, *Fury*, a grim tale of lynch law, in 1936. Sylvia Sidney played the waiflike, vulnerable heroine of *Fury* and would also be the heroine of his next film. Independent producer Walter Wanger asked Lang to direct another social protest film, *You Only Live Once*, a fictionalized version of the criminal career of Bonnie and Clyde.[1] Hollywood gangster movies of the period like *The Public Enemy* emphasize that a gangster's lawless life often began in his misspent youth, and such is the case with *You Only Live Once*. As Lotte Eisner, the foremost Lang scholar, writes, "At sixteen, Eddie Taylor, the male lead, beat up a boy because he sadistically pulled off frogs' legs and was sent to a reformatory. Then, through bad influence of others, and resentment, he began on the downward path."[2]

Wanger brought in Gene Towne and Graham Baker, two witty and intelligent screenwriters, to compose the script. They were known as "two of the most colorful screenwriters in Hollywood."[3] United Artists would distribute the film.

As the screenplay begins, Eddie Taylor (Henry Fonda), a three-time loser, marries Joan Graham (Sylvia Sidney) shortly after serving his third stretch in prison for some petty crimes. Eddie, with Joan's staunch support, is determined to go straight. Father Dolan, played by William Gargan (*The

Story of Temple Drake), says to Eddie on the day he leaves prison, "You don't seem happy for a man that the gates are going to open for." Eddie is sullen because the convicts who bid him good-bye fully expect him to return to jail. The script is suggesting that, while many Americans affirm that a man is innocent until proven guilty, most of the ordinary citizens that Eddie encounters after his release do not believe that at all. But Joan is convinced that the world has a place for them.

Filming was accomplished during November and December 1936. Wanger, an enterprising producer, obtained the services of film editor Daniel Mandell and composer Alfred Newman, who also collaborated on *Dead End*, as did Sylvia Sidney. It was yet another social protest film, as we know. The cinematographer, Leon Shamroy, had done extensive work on documentaries, just the sort of experience that would enable him to give this film a natural look, a fidelity to reality.

On Sylvia Sidney's testimony, Fonda cordially hated Lang. Said Sidney, "Well, Fonda knew that Fritz and I had worked together before" on *Fury*, and "he assumed that Fritz was giving me preferential treatment, giving me extra coaching." Fonda mumbled, "The hell with him! I'll show him!" Sidney concludes, "He gave one hell of a performance."[4]

Fonda resented the number of takes Lang would do before he was satisfied with a scene. As a matter of fact, Lang's meticulous attention to detail earned him the reputation of being a Prussian bully. Hilda Rolfe, his secretary during the 1940s, writes that he responded to such criticism that he was a perfectionist by saying, "and nobody likes a perfectionist."[5] Withal, the picture came in slightly under its budget of $589,403, and Lang delivered the finished film to Wanger in time for its "planned release in late January 1937."[6]

"Of all of Lang's films," Tom Gunning declares in his magisterial biography of the director, "*You Only Live Once* deals most directly with the power of romantic love."[7] Eddie and Joan choose the Valley Tavern Inn for their honeymoon. In the garden of the inn, amid the croaking of frogs, Eddie explains to Joan that "frogs mate for life; if one of them dies, the other dies." They cannot live without one another. Joan adds, "Like Romeo and Juliet." But the inn is not as idyllic a place for lovers as it seems. The newlyweds are routed out of bed in the middle of the night by the husband and wife who run the honeymoon haven. The middle-aged couple informs them that they have learned that Eddie is an ex-convict, so

Fritz Lang going on location for *You Only Live Once* (1937), his first big gangster movie in Hollywood.

he and Joan must vacate the premises immediately. Kate Stables writes in a recent essay on the movie that Eddie is "cast out of society symbolically both by being chased from the honeymoon hotel and by being fired from his job with a trucking firm by his boss who knows of his past."[8]

Sometime later, Monk Mendall, a member of the gang to which Eddie formerly belonged, stages a bank robbery. Monk wears a gas mask during the robbery; he kills a guard while making his getaway in an armored truck through the clouds of smoke from exploding tear-gas bombs. Monk frames Eddie for the armed robbery by leaving behind Eddie's hat, which Monk had stolen from him, and which has Eddie's initials stamped in it. Monk, however, is killed when the truck skids off the road and into a gorge in the middle of a downpour, but Eddie is ultimately convicted of both the robbery and the murder of the guard on circumstantial evidence and given the death penalty.

Joan visits Eddie on Death Row as he waits for his sentence to be carried out. Lang photographs Eddie through the bars of the death cell as he prowls around like a caged animal. When an interviewer told Lang that the weblike shadows of the death cell made it look artificial, Lang countered that the death cell he saw at San Quentin was "reproduced exactly in the film, even with the exact lighting," by Leon Shamroy.[9] Still, Eisner notes that the "dark, heavy bars form a broad, fan-like pattern of shadows."[10]

A lifer with nothing to lose secretly supplies Eddie with a gun with which Eddie can make a break. Gun in hand, Eddie makes his way into the prison courtyard. A thick fog envelops the yard and serves as an apt metaphor for Eddie's foggy state of mind, which renders his perception of the situation hazy. Father Dolan, the prison chaplain, comes forward and attempts to tell Eddie that Monk's corpse has been found in the armored truck at the bottom of a gorge, and so Eddie himself has been pardoned. Dolan instructs the warden, who is standing by, to open the prison gates for Eddie. In his confused state of mind, Eddie does not grasp what is happening; he fires blindly into the fog and accidentally kills Dolan.

Commenting on the unvarnished realism of the film, as exemplified in the way that he staged Eddie's prison break, Lang said, "I think every serious picture [that] depicts people today should be a kind of documentary of its time. Only then, in my opinion, can you get the quality of truth into a picture." He added, "I like to think all of my so-called crime pictures are documentaries."[11]

Joan does not yet know of Eddie's prison break. She is planning to drink poison at the moment of Eddie's execution so that her suicide will coincide with his death, thereby recalling the parable of the frog, whereby when one frog dies, the other will die, too. Eddie phones Joan to tell her of his escape just in time to ward off her suicide.

The film now takes on the resonance of the Bonnie and Clyde saga, as Eddie and Joan take it on the lam together, with a view to crossing the frontier into Canada (not Mexico, as some commentators state). They attain something of the status of legend, as they are assumed to have committed nearly every recent crime in the United States. When they hold up a gas station, just to obtain some gasoline, the two attendants empty the cash register and blame the fugitives.

Joan gives birth to their infant son in a backwoods cabin, but when they leave the nameless baby with her sister, they are recognized and reported by the alert manager of the motel where they are staying. State troopers inevitably catch up with them in the forest just this side of the Mexican border. "The screenplay hits hard," write James Parrish and Michael Pitts, the authors of *The Great Gangster Pictures*, "giving dimension to the story of two hounded . . . souls."[12] One of Shamroy's finest shots shows Eddie and Joan "framed in the cross-hairs of a policeman's gun sight." First Joan is shot, and she dies as Eddie carries her in his arms; then Eddie is mortally wounded.

As Eddie lies dying in the shadowy woods, he sees a vision of heaven and hears the voice of Father Dolan saying, "Eddie, you're free; the gates are open." (This line of dialogue was added by Lang, because it is not in the shooting script.) The huge re-creation of the forest on a studio set, illuminated by dazzling sunbeams miraculously streaming through the branches of the trees, is breathtaking. This image of liberation, epitomized by the priest's saying that the gates are open, represents an ironic contrast to the prison gates that had kept Eddie confined for so long. What's more, we recall Father Dolan saying to Eddie when he was freed from prison at the beginning of the picture that he was a man that the "gates are going to open for"—a line that most commentators overlook.

Stables asks whether the "gates are open," coupled with whether the final shot "is hallucinatory rather than redemptive."[13] Indeed, some critics have wondered if the film's ending is not mere sentimentality. Referring to the strong religious implications of the ending of *You Only Live Once*,

Lang noted, "I was born a Catholic—perhaps I'm not a good Catholic according to the Church—but a Catholic education . . . never leaves you."[14]

There has been a persistent rumor throughout the years that the studio prevailed on Lang to shoot an alternate ending for *You Only Live Once*, lest the overtly religious ending that Lang had provided for the movie did not go down well with the mass audience. According to Sylvia Sidney, "There was never an alternate ending shot for that film. I ought to know; I was there."[15]

Furthermore, Eddie's dying with the promise of eternal life in heaven at film's end recalls Lang's frequent theme: that one who wages a battle against his Fate may lose the struggle, but he may not necessarily be defeated in the long run. Thus, the hero of the present film ultimately conquers Fate by entering the pearly gates with the promise of being united with his beloved beyond the grave. In this context it is worth remembering how Eddie indicated to Joan earlier in the movie that they should not fear death, since they would find one another in the next world, "like Romeo and Juliet."

You Only Live Once is a fairly violent film with a high body count. Nevertheless, Lang thought that the violence he portrayed in films like this one was justified. "I do not use violence for violence's sake," he told me, "but always to illustrate a point or to draw a moral conclusion."[16]

You Only Live Once has maintained a high critical reputation since it was made. Pauline Kael writes, "This early version of the Bonnie and Clyde story, starring Henry Fonda and Sylvia Sidney (neither has ever been better) is certainly one of finest American melodramas of the 1930s."[17] In addition, the film inspired a spate of gangster pictures, so the industry censor, Joseph Breen, sent a warning to the studios that such films are "certain to meet with objections" from church groups and women's clubs.[18]

Hollywood continued to turn out gangster movies for the balance of the 1930s. The Depression ended, and fear of Adolf Hitler replaced fear of Al Capone; so too war pictures replaced gangster movies during World War II. Bogart was no longer playing such gangsters as Baby Face Martin in *Dead End*, but rather heroes the likes of Rick Blaine in *Casablanca* (1942), "enabling him to shed his menacing gangster mantle and become the reluctant hero."[19]

With the end of World War II, war pictures were out and gangster movies were back. Fritz Lang, who made his share of war movies during World War II, for instance, *Hangmen Also Die!* (1943), returned to making gangster films like *The Big Heat*. The gangster pictures of the 1930s depicted policemen fighting criminals; in the postwar era, the "cop rights himself, and cops fight each other," as in *The Big Heat*.[20]

The Big Heat (1953)

Harry Cohn, the chief executive at Columbia Pictures who was so disappointed in Orson Welles's film for Columbia, *The Lady from Shanghai*, welcomed Fritz Lang to the studio to direct *The Big Heat*. The story is based on a serial in the *Saturday Evening Post* by an "excellent crime writer, William McGivern," Lang remembered. He said, "It appealed to me because it combined another struggle against the forces of Fate with a certain social criticism," the exposé of corrupt law enforcement officers and officials.[21] Lang accomplished a "straightforward telling of Sidney Boehm's tightly constructed screenplay."[22] Boehm was a former crime reporter and an experienced screenwriter.

Mike Lagana, the mob boss in *The Big Heat*, tries to avoid stirring up public opinion against organized crime, which has come into the ascendency in postwar America. He does not wish to "wind up in the same ditch with the Lucky Lucianos," as he says in the screenplay. Luciano was a reckless gangster who was deported to Cuba after World War I, and he was a model for Johnny Rocco in *Key Largo*, as we know. Rocco, a holdover from the gangs of the 1930s, could not fit in with the world of organized crime after the war.

The Breen Office, we remember, took a dim view of portraying suicide in a movie, as we know from Breen's complaint about the suicide of Emmerich, as outlined in the script for *The Asphalt Jungle*. After producer Robert Arthur had submitted Sidney Boehm's screenplay for *The Big Heat* to the censor board, he received a letter from Breen's chief consulter, Geoffrey Shurlock, who would replace Breen in a few months, concerning the suicide at the outset of *The Big Heat*. Arthur then sent a memo to Lang in April 1953, stating that the censor's office felt that directly portraying a suicide in the first scene of the script would be too gruesome, and recommending that Lang should not depict the suicide in detail. Lang complied.[23] He spent a month collaborating with Boehm on revisions in the screenplay. In the end, the Mystery Writers of America conferred an Edgar (named for Edgar Allan Poe) on Boehm for the best screenplay of a crime film for 1953.

Lang was also involved in the casting of the major roles. Glenn Ford, Columbia's top leading man since he costarred with Rita Hayworth in *Gilda* in 1946, was selected to play police detective Dave Bannion. Lang chose Gloria Grahame as Ford's costar he said because she "represents today's femme fatale." He continued, "[T]he femme fatale's power over men always comes from a combination of a calculating nature and a glamorous body."[24] Grahame had won an Academy Award for playing a tainted lady in *The Bad and the Beautiful* the previous year. She was a temperamental actress who had several disagreements with Lang on the set, yet her character, a doomed gun moll named Debbie Marsh, gave the film its moral center. Jocelyn Brando, Marlon's sister, plays Dave Bannion's wife Kate.

Gloria Grahame in Fritz Lang's *The Big Heat* (1953), in the role she is most remembered for, gun moll Debbie Marsh.

The director of photography for *The Big Heat* was Charles Lang (*A Foreign Affair*), no relation to the director. Lang gave the movie a documentary-like quality with his spare cinematography, a mastering of darkness and light. Shooting commenced on March 11, 1953, and ran for a mere twenty-eight days. Lang finished in record time because of his careful craftsmanship. Thus, he chose the camera angles in advance and marked them in the margin of his script.

The Breen Office, which thought the original opening shot for the film too gory, should be thanked for influencing Lang to devise an impressive opening shot for the picture. The opening image of the film is that of a .38 revolver lying on a desk. A hand comes into the frame and picks it up. We hear a single shot fired offscreen; then a body slumps forward on the desk. Colin McArthur singles out the film's opening shot as "among the starkest in the cinema," and as a "most appropriate overture" for the violent gangster film to follow.[25]

A sealed letter addressed to the district attorney also lies on the desk, with a police sergeant's badge next to it. The letter, we soon learn, contains Sergeant Tom Duncan's confession of being in the pay of Mike Lagana (Alexander Scourby), a master criminal who dominates the city of Chandlertown. Tom's widow, Bertha (Jeanette Nolan), intends to employ the letter to blackmail Lagana, so she does not turn it over to the police when she finds it, but locks it in a safe instead.

Police sergeant Dave Bannion, in investigating Duncan's suicide, finds out that the dead policeman was involved with Lagana. When Dave goes to Lagana's lavish mansion to question him, the racketeer is outraged that a lowly cop would invade his home to discuss police business. Kim Newman observes that the production designer, Robert Peterson, created sets that fit the personalities of the characters who live there, thus the "tasteless wealth" of Lagana's mansion, with the "jiving teenage party" that his daughter is having for her high school friends when Bannion makes his unwelcome appearance to question her father.[26]

The following night, Bannion's wife Kate is killed when she steps on the starter of the family car and it explodes. The bomb was obviously planted in the family automobile by Lagana's minions and meant for Dave. "Lang achieved one of his most gut-wrenching effects here with a quick, off-camera blast," writes Patrick McGilligan, "focusing instead on Dave's anguished reaction" to his wife's murder.[27] Lang pointed out to me that while *The Big Heat* is a violent film, much of the violence takes place offscreen. That is the case with Tom Duncan's suicide and Kate Bannion's death. Also offscreen is the torture and murder of Lucy Chapman (Dorothy Green), a barfly-cum-hooker who testifies to Dave Bannion that Tom Duncan was on the take from Lagana and had had an affair with her. Lucy's lifeless body is found lying near a county highway. Her death, Bannion notes, was an "old-fashioned, Prohibition-style killing," right out of *The Public Enemy*.

Police Commissioner Higgins orders Dave to terminate the Duncan investigation, since he does not want Duncan's disgraceful association with Lagana to become public knowledge. Dave adamantly refuses to do so and is summarily suspended from the force. The embittered Dave turns in his badge, but not his gun, saying, "the gun is mine, bought and paid for." Dave Bannion is now determined to investigate his wife's death on his own, since he can no longer do so as a law enforcement officer. Gus Burke (Robert Burton), another cop who was Dave's partner, advises him to seek counseling from a priest: "You are on a hate binge." Dave shrugs off Burke's advice; he has become a ruthless avenger, indistinguishable from the gangsters he is pursuing, a theme that resurfaces in *Gangster Squad* (see the afterword).

As the plot unwinds, Dave earns the confidence of Debbie Marsh, the gun moll of Vince Stone (Lee Marvin), Lagana's right-hand man. One of Lagana's henchmen informs Vince that he has seen Debbie conferring with Dave in a bar. Vince later angrily accuses Debbie of two-timing him with Dave. The sadistic brute then throws a pot of scalding coffee in her face, which leaves one side of her face hideously disfigured. Andy Klein singles out this scene as "one of the most shocking scenes in the history of cinema."[28] But, as noted earlier, Lang maintains that he uses violence only to make a point.

In this instance, Lang employs Debbie's disfigured face to symbolize the duality of human nature, that is, an individual's inclination to both good and evil. Debbie's face—one side beautiful, the other side scarred—graphically signifies her capacity for both good and evil. Thus, Debbie, McArthur observes, has become a "two-faced woman," both literally and figuratively. On the one hand, she is good, because she perceives that Bannion is an honorable man, worthy of her help in crusading against

Lagana and his mob. On the other hand, "she is nevertheless morally tarnished . . . by her previous association with Vince Stone and Lagana."[29]

Lang offered an interesting footnote to the filming of the scene just described when he recalled it: "I knew perfectly well that you can throw coffee at someone and not leave a scar at all," because the skin will heal. "So . . . to make the episode more credible, I inserted a shot of the coffee boiling on a hot plate before Vince picked up the pot. That made what happened to Debbie more credible." Novelist William McGivern comments, "It is not the spectacle of scalded, ruined beauty, but the evil of Marvin's face and lips glistening and quivering in Lang's close-up of him, that gives realistic horror to the scene."[30]

Bannion receives word that Commissioner Higgins, who regularly plays poker with Lagana's gang, has called off police protection for Bannion's little daughter Joyce, who is staying in the apartment of Dave's brother-in-law, Al. Dave rushes to Al's apartment building and is accosted by an unidentified stranger stepping out of the shadows on the first-floor staircase. Dave assumes, as does the viewer, that the sinister figure is one of Lagana's gang. In fact, he is one of a group of Al's former army buddies, whom Al has commandeered to protect the child. Out on the street, Dave meets Burke, his erstwhile partner, and his former boss, Lieutenant Ted Wilkes, two policemen who have come to guard the apartment. Dave realizes that he is no longer without friends, as he had thought.

Dave subsequently confesses to Debbie that he nearly strangled Bertha Duncan when he attempted to force her to confess that she had withheld her dead husband's suicide note to blackmail Lagana. Debbie answers, "You couldn't have done it; if you could have, there wouldn't be much difference between you and Vince Stone." The point is that Dave Bannion is not a heartless hoodlum like Vince Stone. He is still a fundamentally decent person and has not degenerated into the kind of cruel, hard-boiled individual that Vince Stone is as a result of seeking revenge for Kate's death. In Dave's case, the capacity for good in his character is still stronger than his capacity for evil.

In an effort to get even with Vince for his cruelty to her, Debbie betrays him and his boss, Lagana, by taking matters into her own hands. Debbie is aware that Bertha Duncan has arranged to have her deceased husband's letter, which contains incriminating evidence about Lagana's crime syndicate, delivered to the district attorney in the event of her death. Consequently, Debbie shoots Bertha dead so that Tom Duncan's letter will automatically come into the hands of the district attorney. Then "the big heat" will be on Lagana and his gang. "The big heat" refers to the "pressure that will finally descend upon the corrupt city and purify it," according to Lang scholar Tom Gunning, with whom I discussed this film.[31]

Debbie then proceeds to Vince's apartment and exacts her personal vengeance on him by hurling scalding coffee in his face. She informs him with maniacal glee that she has murdered Bertha Duncan, exulting, "The lid is off the garbage can!" Vince slays her in retaliation for what she has done—just as Dave, who has had Vince's apartment under surveillance, breaks in. Instead of killing Vince on the spot, Dave declines to take the law into his own hands and turns Vince over to the police.

In the final scene, which serves as an epilogue, Dave is back on the force as a policeman in good standing. Once Dave is "reunited with the police force," writes McArthur in his exemplary monograph on *The Big Heat*, "Bannion's reintegration into society is complete," and he is once more in control of his life.[32] Dave is once again the decent, humane man he was at the beginning of the film. In harmony with the pervasive theme of Lang's films, Dave has been wounded by the hostile forces of Fate, but he eventually emerges from the struggle undefeated. *The Big Heat* was the biggest critical and commercial success of Lang's late career. In addition to the fine acting of Ford and Grahame, the performances of Lee Marvin as the sadistic Vince Stone and Jeanette Nolan as Tom Duncan's wily widow were acknowledged as superior by the critics.

What is unusual about Lang, declares Nick Pinkerton, is the "single-mindedness with which he would continue to impress his unmistakable worldview" on his films throughout his long career, from his early German movies to *The Big Heat*, one of the best of all American gangster pictures.[33]

CHAPTER NINE
THE GODFATHER: PART II

T he focus of the gangster film in the 1950s and thereafter was not the push to the top and the inevitable fall, as in *Little Caesar* and *The Public Enemy*, but the "mundane problems of living legitimately once the top had been reached: the conflict of the old life of crime and the new respectability." Such is the case in *The Godfather: Part II*, as Gerald Mast and Bruce Kawin put it.[1] Paramount Pictures had assumed that the first *Godfather* film would be a routine gangster picture and a modest success.

When *The Godfather* (1971) became a runaway hit, the studio brass insisted that Francis Ford Coppola, its director and cowriter, come up with a sequel. *The Godfather: Part II* would continue to examine organized crime in the 1950s, when the Senate Committee on Organized Crime, chaired by Senator Estes Kefauver, investigated the Syndicate, which is depicted in *The Big Heat*. The term *syndicate* "lacks any ethnic resonance."[2] Nevertheless, in *The Big Heat*, Mike Lagana is portrayed as a first-generation Italian with Old World origins, foreshadowing the Mafia types in the *Godfather* films. In Coppola's Mafia movies, the word *family* is substituted to signify each of the gangs making up the New York Mafia to mollify the coalition of Italian American groups who protested the use of the word *Mafia* in the films.

In approaching the screenplay of *The Godfather: Part II*, Coppola explains, "I thought it would be interesting to juxtapose the ascension of the family under Vito Corleone with the decline of the family under his son Michael, to show in flashback how the young Vito Corleone was building this crime family in America, while his son in the present is presiding over its disintegration."[3] In the documentary that accompanies the *Godfather* trilogy on DVD, Coppola notes, "I had always wanted to write a screenplay that told the story of a father and a son at the same age: They were both in their thirties, and I would integrate the two stories."[4] Young Vito Corleone's early life as an immigrant is set during World War I, while the later life of the Corleone family, presided over by son Michael, is updated to the 1950s. The modern story depicts the family as "beset by Byzantine intrigues, marital discord, fraternal rivalry, and internal decay."[5] Consequently, *The Godfather: Part II* covers nearly sixty years of U.S. history, from the immigrants coming to the United States in the early 1900s until the post–World War II era.

Paramount had commissioned Mario Puzo, author of the novel *The Godfather* (1969), to prepare a preliminary draft of the screenplay before Coppola came on board, and Coppola incorporated some incidents from it in his version of the screenplay. Most of the events in the modern story were invented by Coppola. Some of them were suggested by contemporary newspaper accounts. There is, for example, the incident in which Michael frames Nevada senator Pat Geary by having a dead prostitute found in his bed in a sleazy bordello run by the Corleones to ensure the senator's continued patronage of the Corleone enterprises. This episode was inspired by a sensational newspaper exposé of Nevada brothels.

The flashbacks to young Vito's life in New York's Little Italy were drawn from material left over from Puzo's novel—historical background for which there had been no room in the first film. In fact, part III of the novel is a thirty-page description of the rise of the Mafia in Sicily and Vito Corleone's subsequent rise to power as a Mafia leader when he immigrates to the United States.[6] Puzo chronicles how Vito becomes a Mafia godfather who is a sort of Italian-immigrant entrepreneur in Little Italy. Coppola simply plucked historical incidents from part III of the novel and wrote them into the screenplay.

These flashbacks essentially depict the experiences of immigrants like Vito Corleone coming to the United States and endeavoring to realize the American dream of success, but they were reduced to laboring in sweat shops and dwelling in slum tenements, so they found self-esteem and cash by joining street gangs, which they saw as brotherhoods. The immigrants had a tradition of violence born of their resistance to the rural landlords who had exploited them in Sicily. When they came to the United States, they formed street gangs and secret societies, just as they had done in the old country. Crime became a means of survival in the lawless slums, which were therefore a fertile ground for the growth of the Mafia in the United States.

"My heart was really in the Little Italy sequences," Coppola remembers, "in the old streets of New York, the music, all that turn-of-the-century atmosphere."[7] To that extent, Coppola sees *The Godfather: Part II* as a personal film in which he addresses his own ancestors and ethnic heritage.

Many of the actors from *The Godfather* reprised their roles in *The Godfather: Part II*. Al Pacino, Talia Shire (the director's sister), Diane Keaton, John Cazale, and Robert Duvall returned. Coppola was at pains to find the right actor to play Vito Corleone as a young man. He tested Robert De Niro (*Mean Streets*). "I thought De Niro could be the young Brando," Coppola says in the DVD commentary.[8] He had a sort of stately bearing, as if he really was the young Vito who would grow into the older man who was Marlon Brando in *The Godfather*. By the way, G. D. Spradling, a former politician, was selected to play a politician: Nevada senator Pat Geary.

Al Pacino suggested Lee Strasberg to play crime syndicate treasurer Hyman Roth, an aging Jewish racketeer. Strasberg was head of the renowned Actor's Studio in New York, where he had been Pacino's mentor. Strasberg made Roth a wily financial wizard who was a worthy opponent for Michael. Roth ostensibly treats Michael as an ally but covertly plots to overthrow him. He was modeled on the notorious Jewish gangster Meyer Lansky. Like Lansky, Roth lives in a modest bungalow in Florida, which belies his status as a wealthy, powerful kingpin of organized crime. One gangster warns Michael, "Your father did business with Hyman Roth, but your father never trusted Hyman Roth." At one point, Roth tells Michael that one of his idols is Arnold Rothstein, who fixed the 1919 World Series, a crime that comes up in *The Great Gatsby*.

Coppola brought back some creative personnel who had worked on *The Godfather*. They included cinematographer Gordon Willis, known in Hollywood as the "Prince of Darkness" for his shadowy lighting and penchant for darkened rooms with actors shown in silhouette, and production designer Dean Tavoularis, who won an Academy Award for creating Old New York, Sicily, and Cuba in the film.

Principal photography began on October 28, 1973, and included location work done in Santa Domingo in the Dominican Republic. Santa Domingo was the site chosen for the scenes set in Cuba, where Michael attends a high-level conference with other leaders of organized crime. During the Batista regime in Cuba, the Mafia was involved in the casinos and other rackets there, but their holdings there would soon be lost in the wake of the overthrow of Batista's dictatorship by Fidel Castro, which is portrayed in this sequence.

By May 1974, Coppola had finished principal photography—in 104 days. By November, the rough cut had been pared down to three hours and twenty minutes. Coppola firmly believed that in moving back and forth in time at significant moments in the lives of father and son, he had linked their lives together and showed how each had dealt with problems that faced the family.[9] In switching back and forth from a scene in Michael's time to Vito's young manhood, Coppola took pains to provide smooth transitions between present and past that would suggest the affinities between Michael and his father. Thus, Michael gazes down at his sleeping son in his Tahoe mansion, and the scene slowly dissolves to Vito gazing down at his firstborn son in the same fashion in a New York tenement.

Francis Ford Coppola.

Coppola managed to pull together a final cut of the movie just days before the premiere in December. He had succeeded in creating a vast epic reflecting the development of organized crime in the United States, in terms of the Italian-immigrant past. As Pauline Kael says, "We only saw the middle of the story in the first film; now we have the beginning and the end." The second *Godfather* film not only chronicles Michael's later career as head of the "family business," but it also presents in flashback Don Vito's early life in Sicily, as well as his rise to power in New York City's Little Italy after his immigration to the United States. Kael continues, "The daring of *Part II* is that it enlarges the script and deepens the meaning of the first film."[10]

The parallel structure of the film brings into relief the symbiotic relationship between Vito and Michael. The child Vito Corleone, who arrives at Ellis Island, will grow up to forge a crime family that will "subvert the American dream to attain criminal wealth," and his son Michael will follow in his footsteps.[11] To that extent, *The Godfather: Part II* can be called Coppola's requiem for the American dream.

The Godfather: Part II begins where the previous picture left off, with the scene in which Don Michael's lieutenants pay him homage as his deceased father's rightful successor. Then the movie switches swiftly to a scene from the childhood of Michael's father, when young Vito's own father is murdered for defying Don Ciccio, the local Mafia don in the Sicilian village where Vito was born. Vito's mother and older brother are also murdered shortly thereafter for attempting to take vengeance on the Mafia chieftain, and Vito, now an orphan, escapes to the United States.

In 1901, the child Vito goes through the immigration process at Ellis Island. The wide-eyed Vito Andolini cannot communicate with the American immigration official, so he stands by mutely as the officer mistakenly records his name as Vito Corleone, thereby naming him for his hometown of Corleone. The sallow, frail boy is diagnosed as having contracted small pox and is therefore quarantined for three months on Ellis Island. The lad comes to the United States carrying another sickness as well, that of the vendetta. "The child will carry his vendetta-disease to the point of emerging as a Mafia don and liquidating those who have harmed his family."[12]

Back in the present, the film focuses on another youngster, Michael's son Anthony, who is enjoying a big celebration in honor of his

First Communion. The party is being held at his father's estate at Lake Tahoe, now the center of Michael's business operations. Michael, like his father before him, conducts his business affairs while the festivities are in full swing. While Michael is engaged in making Machiavellian deals in his shadowy study, he is swallowed up in darkness; "his face is often half-lit, his presence tends to recede into the darker parts of the frame," depicting him as an enigma to those he is dealing with.[13] Michael bribes Senator Pat Geary with a large "donation," ostensibly for the state university, but actually to buy Geary's support in securing a gambling license for one of the Corleone Las Vegas casinos. Geary sneers at Michael and his entourage, calling them wops, dagos, and other derogatory names, but he takes the money.

The sacred First Communion ceremony demonstrates the participation by Mafia families in empty displays of religious belief, but they steadfastly ignore the spiritual import of these time-honored religious rituals.[14] The sacrament of Holy Communion does not touch their lives. Like Don Vito before him, Michael deploys Catholic ceremonies to legitimize his lifestyle. The Holy Communion ceremony is followed by a noisy, vulgar outdoor party that demonstrates just how far the Corleone family has drifted from its ethnic origins. "The Italian customs associated with the old country are no longer evident in the scenes set in the modern era," says Coppola.[15] The hearty Italian folk songs have been replaced by suave dance numbers of the big band era.

The drunken Frankie Pentangeli (Michael V. Gazzo), who is from Vito's old neighborhood, disdains the music at the reception, as well as the champagne that has replaced Italian wine. He upbraids Michael for abandoning his roots. Frankie likewise excoriates him for doing business with the "despicable old Jew" Hyman Roth. Michael answers Frankie by saying that his policy is to keep his friends close, but his enemies closer. Frankie, however, does not buy his explanation.

Throughout the party scene, it becomes apparent that the in-laws who have been coming into the Corleone family lately are not of Italian origin and have no sense of the family traditions. Mama Corleone (Morgana King) expresses her displeasure at the diminishing of the family's ethnic identity. Fredo's wife Deanna (Marianna Hill), who is not Italian, is a floozy and a drunk, and she flirts with younger men at the reception. When Fredo (John Cazale) futilely tries to make her behave, she shouts at him about how these "dagos" attempt to dominate their wives. "Never marry a wop!" she bellows, as two of Michael's gang hustle her away from the party.

Since Michael is head of the family, Connie (Talia Shire) goes through the motions of asking his permission to marry a WASP named Merle Johnson (Troy Donahue), whom Michael rightly infers is a fortune hunter. Connie has become a hardened, dissipated creature. Coppola comments on the DVD, "She has these fancy boyfriends; that's the only way she can rebel against her all-powerful brother." The wretched marriages of Fredo and Connie reflect how the "family unity is really starting to break down in this period," concludes Coppola.[16]

After the First Communion reception, the story shifts in due course to a flashback, in which we learn how the Old World criminal traditions imported to the New World add to the misery of struggling immigrants like Vito Corleone. The secret crime cartel called the Black Hand, an early version of the Mafia in the United States, terrorized Italian immigrants living in ethnic neighborhoods by extorting "protection" money from them. The term *Black Hand* referred to crude drawings of a shadowy hand that accompanied threats from these racketeers.

During the performance of an Italian operetta, Genco, Vito's friend points out Fanucci, a Black Hand extortionist, to Vito and warns him that Fanucci extorts protection money from Italian immigrants. Fannuci's florid cape and curled moustache make him look like a villain from a nineteenth-century gaslight melodrama. Vito replies cryptically that Genco should not worry about Fanucci. He says, "I will make him an offer he can't refuse" (a remark that the older Vito makes in *The Godfather* about someone else). When Fanucci periodically attempts to terrorize Vito, his comrades, and their families, Vito finally assassinates him, thereby committing his first murder and committing himself irrevocably to a life of crime. With that, the first part of the picture draws to a close.

Throughout the film, Coppola makes it clear that the higher Michael rises in the hierarchy of Mafia chiefs, the lower he sinks into the depths of moral degradation. As the second part of the film gets under way, Kay (Diane Keaton), Michael's wife, is appalled by what he has become; she finally comes to the bitter conclusion that Michael will never change his ways and phase out his unlawful business interests, as he had promised her so often that he would. Indeed, it is far too late in the day for Michael

Al Pacino as Michael Corleone in *The Godfather: Part II* (1974).

to become a legitimate businessman, even if he wanted to. "He can never go back to the time before . . . he shot his father's enemies," Kael writes. "Michael's act, which preserved his family's power," ruined his own life by setting him on the road to a life of crime.[17]

Michael is subpoenaed to testify before a Senate committee investigating organized crime, and Coppola portrays how adroitly Michael handles himself before the committee. The congressional hearing in the film is modeled on the televised hearings conducted by Senator Kefauver and Senator McClellan in the 1950s and 1960s, respectively. Coppola hired real reporters to play the press corps in this sequence to make it seem more real. Frankie Pentangeli, who has become completely alienated from the Corleone crime family, is the star witness against Michael. When Frankie takes the stand, he sees that Michael has imported Frankie's revered older brother Vincenzo from Sicily to witness his testimony. Acknowledging these old family ties, Frankie fakes an attack of amnesia and withdraws his charges against Michael.

Because Kay is now fully aware that Michael is a hardened criminal, she finally informs him that she is leaving him, and taking their little boy and girl with her. At the climax of their dreadful quarrel, Kay reveals that the miscarriage she had told Michael she had suffered earlier was actually an abortion. She killed their unborn son, she explains, because she refused to bring another child into the vicious Corleone world. Michael is shocked to learn of the death of a second son, who would have helped to keep the Corleone name alive. He angrily slaps his wife, knocking her down. But it is Kay who has inflicted the severest blow. Michael orders Kay to get out but leave their two children behind. Coppola comments in his commentary, "Kay is appalled that Michael had gone scot-free after the Senate investigation." She shouts, "I had an abortion, like our marriage is an abortion, something unholy." She explains that what she has done is her way of "resisting the terrible evil that is spreading out from the man she had loved." She knew he would never forgive her, and she wanted out of a Mafia marriage. She is no longer married to the mob.

The second half of the movie continues to develop two separate story lines by showing both young Vito and Michael exacting revenge for earlier treachery. We watch Vito return briefly to the Sicily of his boyhood to stab to death Don Ciccio, the local Mafia chieftain responsible for the deaths of his parents and brother decades before. Don Ciccio is an aging, decrepit man at this point, so Vito's gruesome vendetta-killing of the pathetic don, a crime committed with ruthless premeditation, illustrates the savage side of Vito's nature that lurks beneath the charming and civilized façade that he cultivates.

In a parallel act of vengeance, Michael arranges for the assassination of rival mobster Hyman Roth, who had plotted to have Michael slain. Michael has no sympathy for Roth: "He's been dying of the same heart attack for twenty years." Michael also orders that his weak and ineffectual older brother Fredo should be shot when he learns that Fredo, who all along had been jealous of his kid brother Michael for superseding him as head of the Corleone family, had cooperated with Roth's scheme to murder Michael. Coppola notes that Puzo states in the novel that, "revenge is a dish best served cold."

In the film, Michael decides to spare Fredo while Mama Corleone is still matriarch of the family. At her mother's wake, Connie, who is no longer the brazen hussy she was at the beginning of the movie, entreats Michael to forgive Fredo's treachery. While Michael embraces Fredo in a spurious gesture of fraternal affection, he glares at Al Neri, Michael's enforcer, thereby signaling to him that the time to take vengeance on Fredo is at hand. The murder occurs when Fredo goes fishing just off the pier from Michael's Tahoe estate. Fredo says a "Hail Mary" to ensure that he will catch a fish. It is the last prayer he will ever utter.

Coppola had Willis film the scene in which Neri liquidates Fredo in long shot to show how it looked from Michael's point of view as he witnessed the killing through the Venetian blinds in his office. When Fredo is killed, the stony figure of Michael stands gazing out of a window in the family compound. His transformation to moral monster is now complete; he has lost his moral compass and may never find it again.

Once Michael has become permanently alienated from his wife, he is left a lonely, disconsolate man, living in virtual isolation in his heavily guarded compound at Lake Tahoe. Michael may have built the Corleone family into one of the strongest Mafia clans in the United States, but he has, at the same time, lost most of his immediate family: he murdered his only remaining brother, and he has banished his wife. Michael has always maintained that the harsh measures he has taken were motivated by his determination to protect his family, and the fortified compound where they live is a grim physical emblem of that commitment.[18] Yet, by film's end, the vile family business has invaded his home and all but destroyed it. As Talia Shire puts it, "Francis felt that he had to knock this family off to show how their criminal activities destroyed the family."[19]

Even though Frankie Pentangeli had recanted his intention to testify against him, Michael is convinced that he should pay for his original willingness to do so. He sends Tom Hagen (Robert Duvall), Mafia consigliore (family lawyer) and adopted son of Vito Corleone, to visit Frankie, who is still in the FBI's witness protection program and living at an army base. How a Mafia consigliore gained access to Frankie while he is sequestered in an army compound is never explained. In any case, Tom has a discussion with Frankie about how traitors were dealt with during the days of the Roman Empire—which is, after all, the structural model for the Mafia. Tom says, "If they committed suicide, their families were taken care of by the Roman regime."[20] Coppola affirms that Puzo wrote this scene based on the old Roman idea that a man's family would be spared if he did the right thing and opened his veins and bled to death in the bathtub. Frankie obliges, and his demise is a "Roman death."

The climactic sequence at the end of *The Godfather: Part II*, in which Michael's principal enemies die in a series of vignettes, recalls a similar montage at the conclusion of *The Godfather*. In quick succession, Frankie Pentangeli slashes his wrists in the bathtub at the army base. Hyman Roth is assassinated at an airport as he is interviewed by reporters. And Fredo is shot in a rowboat while fishing on the Tahoe estate. Comments Coppola, "There's no doubt that by the end of this picture, Michael Corleone, having beaten everyone, is sitting alone, a living corpse."

The final image of Michael sitting in a thronelike chair on the lawn of his estate on a bleak autumn afternoon, brooding over the loss of many members of his family, recalls the shot in the film's first flashback, in which the sickly young Vito Corleone sits in an enormous chair in a lonely hospital room at Ellis Island right after his arrival in the New World. The lad, we know, came to the United States because of a vendetta against his family in his own country, and he will grow up to wreak vengeance on the man who slaughtered his loved ones back home.[21]

Years later, his son Michael will, in turn, take it upon himself to avenge a murderous attack on his father's life. By so doing, he will inevitably become an integral part of the ongoing pattern of vengeance that began with the massacre of his ancestors long before he was born. Hence, there is a direct connection between the frail little boy sitting alone in the oversized chair at the beginning of the movie and his grown son sitting alone in a majestic chair late in the movie. Coppola articulates that connection in his remark that in *The Godfather: Part II*, his purpose was to "show how two men, father and son, were . . . corrupted by this Sicilian waltz of vengeance."[22] Revenge, as noted earlier, is a dish best served cold.

The last major flashback takes place at the outbreak of World War II, December 7, 1941, just after the Japanese attack on Pearl Harbor. The Corleone family, including Sonny (James Caan), Fredo, Connie, and Tom, are waiting for Don Vito to come home for a surprise birthday party in his honor. Michael takes the occasion to announce that he has enlisted in the U.S. Marines. The volatile Sonny (who is killed in *The Godfather*) chides Michael for risking his life for strangers, while Tom says on Vito's behalf, "Your father has plans for you." The final flashback concludes as the family runs out of the room to greet Vito—except for Michael, who is left sitting alone at the dining room table. He is already a loner who will live his life his own way.

In the movie's last shot of Michael, he is ironically still wearing his wedding ring. It is an empty symbol of his pose as a family man, for he is as alone at this moment as was the boy Vito in the quarantine cell on Ellis Island. In contemplating Michael at film's end, one recalls what Robert Warshow says in his seminal essay on the gangster film: "The typical gangster film represents a steady upward progress, followed by a very precipitous fall."[23] Coppola adds, Michael "is prematurely old, like the hero of *The Picture of Dorian Gray*."[24]

When *The Godfather: Part II* came out, some critics wrote it off as a mere rehash of *The Godfather*. Still, other critics were enthusiastic, according to Rodney Hill in *The Francis Ford Coppola Encyclopedia*: A. D. Murphy says in *Variety*, "*Godfather II*, far from being a spin-off follow-up to its 1972 progenitor, is an excellent epochal drama in its own right."[25] Kael cheers, "The sensibility at work here is that of a major artist. . . . The film is a modern American epic."[26]

On Oscar night, Coppola became one of the few filmmakers in cinema history to win the triple crown: he received Academy Awards for directing the picture, coauthoring the screenplay, and producing the best picture of the year. Indeed, *The Godfather: Part II* is the first sequel to win Best Picture. Robert De Niro won an Oscar for his supporting role as young Vito. He delivered most of his lines in Sicilian—a language he did not understand. In addition, Nino Rota and Carmine Coppola (the director's father) won Oscars for the musical score. Ironically, Pacino was nominated but did not win an Oscar. Yet, Michael Corleone is still considered Pacino's greatest role, "because Michael is one of the few movie characters to achieve an authentically tragic dimension."[27] In sum, *The Godfather: Part II* remains one of the greatest gangster pictures ever made.

CHAPTER TEN

BONNIE AND CLYDE AND
THE UNTOUCHABLES

Bonnie and Clyde (1967)

The gangster picture continued to develop in the 1960s and 1970s, after the success of *The Big Heat* in the 1950s. The contrast between crime movies set in the city and those set in the country began to emerge. This distinction served to define the difference between urban criminals and rural criminals. When Robert Warshow stated in "The Gangster as Tragic Hero" that gangsters belonged to the city, one wondered what he would have made of *Bonnie and Clyde*, which clearly portrayed rural criminals. "Arthur Penn's flamboyant, affecting, and ultimately tragic saga of a pair of Depression-era gangsters" set new standards for on-screen violence.[1]

At the time when Lang made *You Only Live Once*, his fictionalized version of Bonnie Parker and Clyde Barrow (see chapter 8), Sylvia Sidney recalled that the "papers were full of them, with that famous picture of Bonnie with her foot on the running board of the car, holding a tommy gun and smoking a cigar."[2] Penn's much more realistic and authentic film would bring Bonnie and Clyde back to the public's attention.

When the movie premiered in August 1967, it was a resounding failure. "Warren Beatty came under fire for *Bonnie and Clyde*," for which he was both producer and star, "because it was considered sensationalistic and was pilloried for glamorizing violence."[3] Beatty contended that the movie failed because Warner Bros. gave it a limited release due to the fact that Jack Warner had expressed great dissatisfaction with it.

Still, Jack Warner was on the verge of retirement as studio chief, so, at Beatty's behest, Warner took the unprecedented step of relaunching the movie two months later with a fresh ad campaign. Beatty was convinced that although the picture had gotten some hostile reviews, it had been embraced by younger moviegoers who resonated with Bonnie and Clyde's antiauthority, antiestablishment views. In fact, Penn's movie had helped to identify a previously untapped market of young people who were fed up with the "beach party movies" that the studios had been feeding them in recent years, and who gravitated toward the youthful counterculture, of which Warner's own *Rebel without a Cause* (1955) was a harbinger. Furthermore, the movie reaffirmed the image of the gangster as a "heroic loner," an image that had flourished in the gangster pictures of the 1930s, starring James Cagney and Edward G. Robinson.[4]

The original screenplay for *Bonnie and Clyde* was the work of two neophyte scriptwriters, David Newman and Robert Benton. (Benton would later write and direct his own screenplays, e.g., *Places in the Heart*.) Beatty got Arthur Penn to direct the picture because he had already collaborated with Penn on a crime drama, *Mickey One* (1965). Penn asked for some changes in the screenplay. "We weren't making a documentary," he explained; "to some extent we did romanticize the main characters, but so, inevitably, does any storyteller."[5] The screen-writers went with the Barrow family's image of Clyde as a charming young man who possessed little respect for the law and felt justified in pulling the trigger whenever he felt cornered. He idolized Jesse James and convinced himself and Bonnie that they were champions of the poor and downtrodden during the Depression. By the same token, "they were regarded as folk heroes by many people," said Penn, even though they killed at least sixteen people, half of whom were law enforcement officers. Penn was dramatizing their legend, what he called the "mythic aspect of their lives."[6]

The historical Clyde Barrow, by all accounts, was homosexual, but Penn prevailed on the scriptwriters to make him impotent, a problem that would not complicate Clyde's relationship with Bonnie as much as homosexuality would. (In real life, they apparently had a young man with them that was bisexual and "serviced" both Bonnie and Clyde, or so it was rumored.) The young man, who is a member of their gang in the movie, is straight: C. W. Moss, as he is called in the script, is a combination of two young men who were members of the gang, which helped to simplify the plot. Their real names were William Daniel Jones and Henry Methvin (whose father eventually betrayed Bonnie and Clyde to the police).

Beatty originally wanted Shirley MacLaine, his sister, to play Bonnie, but he finally settled on Faye Dunaway, who was not a movie star when she took the part. But costume designer Theodora Van Runkle (*The Godfather: Part II*) catapulted her to fame by designing clothes for her that had the "retro" look of 1930s fashions, topped off by a rakish beret that became a fad with younger women.

Another member of the creative team was director of photography Burnett Guffey (*From Here to Eternity*). With a minimum of light, Guffey was adept at conjuring up a "naturalistic, gritty look, to complement hard-boiled stories of criminals."[7] When the front office at Warner Bros. complained loudly that some scenes in *Bonnie and Clyde* were too dark, Guffey was offended and walked off the picture for a week in protest, but he came back and finished the picture and went on to win an Academy Award for his cinematography in the film.

Guffey's filming of the family reunion, when Bonnie and Clyde visit her mama and kinfolk, is masterful. Bonnie's interchange with her mother recalls that of Baby Face Martin (Humphrey Bogart) and his mother (Marjorie Main) in *Dead End* (see chapter 4). Penn told Guffey that he wanted the family scene to have a soft-focused look, and Guffey obliged by putting a piece of window screen over the camera lens to achieve a gauzy, nostalgic effect.

"The editing of this movie," writes Kael in her extended review of the film, "is the best editing in an American movie in a long time."[8] The editor, Dede Allen, combined a classical Hollywood editing style with more modern techniques, for instance, the jump cut, "giving the film a jagged, menacing quality."[9] There is, for example, the quick look of panic that Bonnie and Clyde exchange just before the Texas Rangers ambush them. Allen would continue to collaborate with Penn after the present movie.

A revised Motion Picture Production Code was promulgated by the Motion Picture Association of America (MPAA), replacing the original code of 1930, on September 20, 1966. It was designed to "keep in harmony with the mores, culture, moral sense, and expectations of our society."[10] As a result, movies like *Bonnie and Clyde* could receive the seal of approval, which would have been unlikely under the previous code.

The opening credits feature actual family snapshots of Bonnie and Clyde taken before they met. This forecasts what the film proper will take up after the credits, with their first meeting: Looking through her bedroom window, Bonnie Parker spies a young man endeavoring to break into her mother's automobile. She rushes down to the sidewalk and confronts one Clyde Barrow, who contends that her assumption that he was attempting to steal her mother's Tin Lizzie was all a misunderstanding. He introduces himself as a former convict and proficient thief. He shows off his gun, which serves as a phallic symbol. She fondles his weapon and says, "I'll bet you're not man enough to use it," thereby prefiguring the scene in which she will discover that he is impotent. Clyde demonstrates his abilities as a thief by holding up a nearby grocery store and stealing a getaway car for good measure. He then invites her to join him in a life of unpredictable adventure.

While engaging in target practice in the front yard of a ramshackle house, a farmer and his family drive up in a truck weighed down with all their worldly possessions; they want to take a last look at their farm, which has been repossessed by the bank. As a gesture of sympathy, Clyde puts a bullet in the bank's foreclosure sign. As the farmer and his family are about to leave, Clyde suddenly boasts, "We rob banks!" Comments Leland Poague, "He hasn't robbed one yet, but he's committed to trying."[11]

Penn injects humor into the film at times to offset the violence. While Clyde is holding up a grocery store to get a supply of food, the manager attacks him with a meat cleaver. Clyde runs out the door, shouting at Bonnie, "Try to get something to eat and the sonofabitch comes at you with a meat cleaver! I didn't want to hurt him!"

While getting gas at a run-down gas station, they recruit C. W. Moss (Michael J. Pollard), the attendant, to be their driver and mechanic. He is a graduate of a reform school and does not hesitate to join up with gangsters to continue his life of crime.

When the gang is escaping from a bank they just robbed, the bank manager recklessly jumps on the running board of their car. Clyde, caught off guard, fires his pistol at the man's face, putting out his eye, thereby spraying the car window with blood. At that moment, we realize, Bonnie and Clyde are no longer "adventurers," but full-fledged gangsters playing for keeps.

Faye Dunaway and Warren Beatty as gangster lovers in Arthur Penn's *Bonnie and Clyde* (1967).

Clyde's older brother Buck (Gene Hackman, in a terrific perfor-mance) and his flighty wife Blanche (Estelle Parsons) join the Barrow gang. Bonnie objects, but Clyde insists that they are family. The impor-tance of family seems to mean as much to these impecunious hillbillies as it does to the Mafia. At any rate, the Barrow gang captures a Texas Ranger, Frank Hamer (Denver Pyle). Bonnie suggests that they make him pose for a photo with all of them, "looking as friendly as pie," and then send the snapshot to the press. The taciturn Hamer appears to be deeply offended by being forced to pose with gangsters, and one surmises that he will not rest until he gets even with Bonnie and Clyde to salvage his professional standing as a law enforcement officer.

For his part, Clyde is chagrined when the papers print spurious ac-counts of the Barrow gang reportedly carrying out robberies in Illinois, Indiana, and New Mexico—states they have never been to.

During their next bank robbery, Clyde asks a customer, "Is that your money or the bank's?" He replies that it is his; Clyde responds, "You keep it then." This brief encounter shows how Bonnie and Clyde encourage their public image as Robin Hoods who rob the rich to give to the poor. Obviously they rob the rich, but they seldom give any of what they steal to the poor. They scoop up their take from a bank robbery and pile into their getaway car, which is a Tin Lizzie. Then they take off down a dusty country road to the tune of Flatt and Scruggs's exuberant banjo plunking, which makes the policemen, who are in hot pursuit in their jalopy, seem like Keystone Kops.

Bonnie insists that she visit her mama one last time, so the gang arranges for a family picnic with the Parkers. Clyde reassures Bonnie's mother that he and Bonnie intend to give up their lawless ways "when hard times is over." Mrs. Parker throws cold water on Clyde's fancies by saying, "You'd best keep runnin', Clyde Barrow; and you know it."

In one of the Barrow gang's last skirmishes with the law, Buck is slain when half of his head is blown away, while Blanche is wounded and captured, and consigned to the local prison hospital. Bonnie composes a doggerel ballad, which she reads to Clyde before mailing it to the newspapers. Its conclusion actually foretells their end:

> Someday they'll go down together,
> They'll bury them side by side.
> To a few it'll be grief,
> To the law a relief;
> But it's death for Bonnie and Clyde.

Clyde murmurs when he hears the ballad, "You have made me somebody they're gonna remember." The pair begins to make love, and succeed, as Clyde's impotence has evaporated. Their mutual relationship is the only thing they have left to cling to in life.

Meanwhile, C. W. Moss's father cuts a deal with Texas Ranger Hamer, whereby he will betray Bonnie and Clyde to the law, in exchange for amnesty for his son. Hamer sets up an ambush on a rural road near Arcadia, Louisiana, on May 23, 1934. Thus writes Peter Biskind in his 2010 obituary of Arthur Penn, "The violent, shocking, and justly celebrated fusillade of gunfire that ends the saga of the outlaw couple, sending them into a slow motion dance of death, was all Penn. It was a visual tour de force executed with four cameras running at different speeds."[12] The ballet of bullets, which seems to go on for an eternity, actually lasts only thirty-five seconds, but it sweeps Bonnie and Clyde into the everlasting realm of legend.

Bonnie and Clyde garnered a passel of mixed reviews when it premiered in the summer of 1967. Bosley Crowther, who maligns the picture as a cheap piece of filmmaking in the *New York Times*, was, in due course, kicked upstairs by the *Times* for being out of touch with contemporary tastes. *Newsweek* critic Joseph Morgenstern vilified the movie in his original review, which he recanted in a follow-up notice. *Time* magazine's Jay Cocks excoriated the movie in his review, which he then had to withdraw when the picture became the subject of a *Time* cover story. The article calls the film a "cultural phenomenon," whose chief characters America's alienated younger generation could identify with. To top the critical about-face that marked the picture's opening, Pauline Kael's lengthy *New Yorker* defense of the film came along in October, when the movie was relaunched.

But perhaps the biggest surprise among the picture's defenders was the endorsement from the National Catholic Office for Motion Pictures (NCOMP), formerly the Catholic Legion of Decency, a name the organization shed in 1965, because it smacked of vigilantism. In February 1968, NCOMP held its annual prize-giving ceremony in New York City. NCOMP accorded *Bonnie and Clyde* its citation as the most highly recommended motion picture of 1967. I attended the ceremony, as did the picture's producer, Warren Beatty, and its director, Arthur Penn. Penn told me that he was delighted that NCOMP recognized that *Bonnie and Clyde* was designed to be a thought-provoking work of art and not just a lurid gangster flick.

Anthony Schillaci, an NCOMP consulter, wrote of *Bonnie and Clyde*, "The banality of their evil, compounded of boredom and meaningless lives . . . and the social disorder of the Depression, makes Bonnie and Clyde tragic folk heroes with whom we can identify."[13] *Bonnie and Clyde* won Oscars for Estelle Parsons and Burnett Guffey. It also solidified Arthur Penn's reputation as a major film director. As Jack Shadoian puts it, "*Bonnie and Clyde* is one of the most important and popular films of the 1960s."[14]

Bonnie and Clyde was released at a time when a string of pseudohistorical biographies of gangsters was coming out of Hollywood, from Joseph Newman's *King of the Roaring Twenties: The Story of Arnold Rothstein*

(1961) to Robert Benton's *Billy Bathgate* (1991), with Dustin Hoffman as Dutch Schultz. Al Capone had surfaced in several gangster films, from a fictionalized version of him in *Little Caesar* and *Key Largo* to Richard Wilson's more factual biopic, *Al Capone* (1959), with Rod Steiger as "Scarface" Al Capone (Capone earned the nickname when he was slashed on the face during a knife fight as a kid). The best picture in which Capone figured was Brian De Palma's *The Untouchables*.

The Untouchables (1987)

Alphonse Capone was born in Brooklyn, New York, in 1899—not in Italy, as some other Mafia mobsters were.[15] He moved to Chicago after a misspent youth as a petty crook. He eventually became the undisputed head of the Chicago Syndicate after he had seven members of his gang, dressed as cops, eliminate several rival mobsters in the St. Valentine's Day Massacre in 1929. He was convicted of tax evasion in October 1932, and sentenced to a prison term at Alcatraz in San Francisco Bay. He was released in January 1939, because he was suffering from a case of advanced syphilis that afflicted his brain, as well as other organs.

The TV series *The Untouchables* (1957–1963) stars Robert Stack as Eliot Ness, the federal agent who was charged with bringing down Capone. The series was derived from Ness's biography, which was written by journalist Oscar Fraley, with Ness's cooperation. The series went well beyond the Ness biography to present fictional material needed to fill out six seasons. Thus, in some of the episodes, Ness tangles with the likes of "Legs" Diamond, a gangster he never clashed with in real life. Still, the narration is delivered by newspaper columnist Walter Winchell, whose machine-gun delivery makes the episodes seem like the Gospel truth, when some of them are not.

Capone is dispatched to Alcatraz early in the first season. Hence, Frank Nitti (Bruce Gordon) is Ness's adversary in most of the episodes, since Nitti took over the management of Capone's criminal activities when Capone went to prison. (Nitti is killed by Ness during the course of the 1987 movie *The Untouchables*, which also mixes some fiction with fact.)

The two-hour pilot of *The Untouchables* was released as a feature film in 1962, entitled *The Scarface Mob*, with Neville Brand as Capone. Because of the popularity of the TV series, to which Paramount owned the rights, the studio decided to make a feature film with the same title as the TV series in 1987. Producer Art Linson commissioned Pulitzer Prize–winning playwright and screenwriter David Mamet, who wrote the script for the Paul Newman vehicle *The Verdict* (1982). Mamet fashioned the screenplay of *The Untouchables* as the story of a federal agent who comes to town and meets a policeman, Jimmy Malone. The veteran cop teaches him some tricks about police work, specifically how to get Capone.

Brian De Palma, the film's director, was known for his ingenious thrillers, one example being *Dressed to Kill* (1980), and *The Untouchables* is a superior crime movie. Kevin Costner's career-making performance as dedicated lawman Eliot Ness is buttressed by Sean Connery's portrayal of Jimmy Malone, one of Chicago's honest Irish cops. Robert De Niro gained thirty pounds to enact the role of Al Capone. Although De Niro is only in a few scenes, he dominates every one of them by his menacing demeanor. "The well-dressed sociopath's capacity for murderous blood-shed is always there."[16]

The picture ends with the customary statement that the characters are "purely fictitious," and not based on real people, living or dead. That is a curious statement about a film in which, for a start, Eliot Ness, Al Capone, and Frank Nitti appear with their real names. Moreover, accountant Oscar Wallace is based on Frank Wilson, the real-life accountant who provided the documentation that enabled Ness to convict Capone of tax evasion.

Pointing up Patrizia von Brandenstein's production design in his review of the movie, Roger Ebert writes, "There's a shot of the canyon of La Salle Street, all decked out with 1920s cars and extras, that's sensational. And a lot of nice touches like Capone's hotel headquarters."[17] The exterior of the Lexington Hotel, where Capone lives, was actually the façade of a venerable building at Roosevelt University in downtown Chicago. First-class cinematographer Stephen Burum, who photographed Francis Ford Coppola's *Rumble Fish* (1983) in black-and-white, wanted to film *The Untouchables* in black-and-white as well, but the studio would not hear of it.

De Palma chose Ennio Morricone to compose the background score. Morricone's reputation had been built on scoring such "spaghetti westerns" as *A Fistful of Dollars* (1964) in his native Italy. The indefatigable Morricone tried out several possible themes for the opening credits of

The Untouchables, with pulsating rhythms, before he was satisfied. His imaginative background music matches the violence, emotions, and dark humor of the film.

De Palma's picture begins with a printed prologue: "1930. Prohibition had transformed Chicago into a city at war. Rival gangs competed for control of the city's illegal alcohol. . . . It is the time of gangsters like Al Capone." In the first scene, we see Capone holding court in his hotel suite while he dishes out clichés to reporters: "You will get farther with a kind word and a gun than with a kind word alone." He continues, "People are gonna drink. In making liquor available to the public, I am respecting the will of the people."

Soon thereafter, we see Eliot Ness of the Treasury Department being introduced to the local press and vowing to enforce Prohibition as the "law of the land." Kevin Costner said that he saw Ness not as a "flashy guy," but as a "stable guy" who is determined to catch Capone. Ness recruits three men for his task force: Jimmy Malone (Sean Connery), an Irish cop with many years of experience on the force; George Stone (Andy Garcia), an Italian American anxious to improve the image of Chicago Italians, which has been sullied by Capone and his Mafia mob; and Oscar Wallace (Charles Martin Smith), an accountant who repeatedly reminds Ness that he can nail Capone for tax evasion because Capone has not paid his taxes since 1926.

Malone surreptitiously meets with Ness in a church (Connery's suggestion for the script) so that the Chicago cops on Capone's payroll are unable to eavesdrop on their conversation. Malone's advice to Ness: "He pulls a knife, you pull a gun. He sends one of yours to the hospital, you send one of his to the morgue. That's the Chicago way, and that's the way we'll get Capone!" The "Chicago way" seems to be to fight fire with fire.

After Ness executes a successful brewery raid on a Capone warehouse, Capone has a dinner meeting with his top gang members. "De Palma's visual panache is never more striking than in the banquet scene, when De Niro's Capone caps a dinner speech with a few fatal swings of a baseball bat," aimed at one of Capone's henchmen, who did not short-circuit Ness's raid on Capone's brewery.[18] Capone comments to those present that the guy was not a team player. By contrast, Ness's three comrades are nothing if not team players.

Andy Garcia, Sean Connery, Kevin Costner, and Charles Martin Smith in Brian De Palma's *The Untouchables* (1987).

Later, Alderman John O'Shea (Del Close) attempts to bribe Ness with an envelope filled with money to lay off the Capone gang. Ness refuses the payoff by throwing the envelope in O'Shea's face. O'Shea declares, "You fellows think you are untouchable, but everybody can be gotten to." Shortly afterward, Frank Nitti (Billy Drago), Capone's enforcer, threatens Ness's family. Earlier, during a confrontation in the lobby of Capone's hotel, Capone had shouted at Ness, "Fuck you and fuck your family!" So Ness sends his wife, his little girl, and his infant son away for safekeeping. Family is a key concept in the movie: aside from his wife and children, Ness has another family, his comrades in the Untouchables.

Ness gets wind of a cargo of whiskey being shipped from Canada to Chicago. He alerts the Canadian Mounties and heads with his team to the Canadian border. Ness and his men bide their time in a cabin near the border. Ness shoots one of Capone's gang dead on the porch of the cabin in the opening exchange of gunfire. Inside the cabin, Malone endeavors to get another of Capone's mobsters, who does not know that the first man is dead, to spill what he knows about Capone's rackets, but the second mobster refuses. Malone goes out on the porch, grabs the corpse, props it up against a wall, and says he is going to shoot the guy if he doesn't talk. Malone then puts a gun in the corpse's mouth and pulls the trigger. Inside the cabin the other mobster decides to talk. Malone's quick, brutal action demonstrates that he is aware that "law enforcement is beginning to resemble gang warfare."[19]

In reprisal, Capone orders Nitti to murder two of Ness's team. (In reality, Ness had ten men on his team, and one was killed by a Capone mobster; in the film, Eliot Ness has four men, and two of them are killed.) In the movie, Nitti shoots Wallace while disguised as a policeman (thus recalling the St. Valentine's Day Massacre) in an elevator. Nitti also shoots Malone through a window in his apartment with a double-barreled shotgun. Ness finds the fatally wounded Malone just before he expires. An Irish Catholic, Malone bestows on Ness his medal of St. Jude, patron of lost causes. Ness will subsequently pass the medal on to George Stone, an Italian Catholic.

Capone, in due time, is put on trial for tax evasion; Ness learns that Capone's bookkeeper, Walter Payne (Jack Kehoe), is taking the midnight train to Miami to avoid testifying about Capone's finances. Ness takes Stone along with him to Union Station to intercept Payne so that he will have to appear in open court at the Capone trial. In the script, the railway station sequence, in which Ness and Stone track down Payne, involves a train wreck, but that proved to be too expensive. So De Palma dreamed up an alternate version of the Union Station sequence that is not in the shooting script. Part of it was suggested by Sergei Eisenstein's classic Russian silent film *Potemkin* (1925).

In the sequence in Eisenstein's *Potemkin*, which is called "The Odessa Steps," Russian soldiers massacre peaceful demonstrators on the outdoor staircase near the city of Odessa. During the course of the slaughter, the mother of an infant is killed, and the baby carriage rolls down the steps, with no one to protect the baby.[20] Similarly, in *The Untouchables*, Ness and Stone open fire on the gangsters who are guarding Walter Payne. When the shooting starts, a mother loses her hold on her baby carriage. "De Palma uses the station's enormous staircase to recreate the drama of a baby carriage tumbling down the stairs while caught in a cross fire." The director employs slow motion intermittently throughout the sequence to make the gun battle more riveting. "Ennio Morricone had the idea of using a child's music box to provide the background music for the baby carriage slipping down the steps," De Palma recalls.[21] Neither the baby nor its mother stops a bullet in De Palma's film.

After the shootout, Ness and Stone arrest Payne, who swears he will testify in court about the covert payoffs to Capone in his ledger, for which Capone never paid taxes. After Capone's trial has concluded, Ness shouts at him in the courtroom, "Never stop fighting until the fight is over"—a motto he lives by. Ness follows Nitti to the roof of the courthouse to arrest him. Nitti sneers at Ness that Capone's henchmen will see to it that the murder charges against him for killing Malone and Wallace will not stick. Ness goes berserk at the thought of Nitti walking away from the slayings of Ness's comrades. He gets even with Nitti by hurling Nitti's body "from the building, and it is pulverized as it crashes through the roof of a car."[22]

In throwing Nitti off the roof, Ness is taking the law into his own hands. This implies how a law enforcement officer risks being tainted with the corruption of the gangsters he is pursuing. In actual fact, Ness did not kill Nitti, who shot himself in 1943, after being indicted for extortion and mail fraud.[23] Asked why the scene of Nitti's death is in the film, De Palma replied that he wished to show that the "gory deaths of Malone and Wallace motivate Ness to do things he never thought he could do. Also, Nitti being pushed off the roof allows the audience to savor a really bad guy being killed."

Just before the final fadeout, a cub reporter buttonholes Ness on the street and inquires what he will do when Prohibition is repealed. He answers laconically, "I think I'll have a drink." The cognoscenti would know that Ness became an alcoholic after he moved to Cleveland later on, and an investigator for the Cleveland police force. He was involved in a hit-and-run accident while under the influence of liquor and forced to retire.[24] But most people who see the film would not know of Ness's inglorious end. Little wonder that he met Oscar Fraley, who would write his biography, in a bar.

As the viewer watches Eliot Ness stride down La Salle Street at film's end, Ness is having his moment of fame. *The Untouchables* was also Brian De Palma's moment of fame. The movie received accolades from critics and was a triumph at the box office. Although De Palma made some more good films, he never again made another film as good as *The Untouchables*.

CHAPTER ELEVEN
THE GRIFTERS AND *THE DEPARTED*

The Grifters (1990)

Mafia top guns like Al Capone were tough bosses of organized crime in the 1930s and 1940s, but as time went on, smarter, slicker crime bosses were moving in on the rackets. In the 1950s and thereafter, gangsters learned that such old-style mobsters as Johnny Rocco in *Key Largo* were no longer shrewd enough to control a gang. Then there were the grifters, who, like the poor, we always have with us. A grifter is a small-time swindler who lacks the intelligence or experience to be successful in the world of organized crime.

Jim Thompson, author of *The Grifters* (1963), which Stephen Frears filmed in 1990, was the author of several hard-boiled pulp fiction novels dealing with violent and self-destructive antiheroes and antiheroines. He possessed a genuine ear for dialogue, which should have made his books attractive to Hollywood, but his dark, nihilistic vision, which filmmakers saw as gloomy, scared them off. Thompson was a hopeless alcoholic, and alcoholics are notorious for their pessimistic view of life. Stephen King once said of Thompson, "He went running into the American subconscious with a blowtorch in one hand and a pistol in the other, screaming his goddamn head off. No one else came close" to writing such uncompromising hard-boiled fiction the way he did.[1] Thompson excelled at writing about sweaty, desperate characters on the margins of society, characters whom he first observed as a youngster, working as a bellhop in a tawdry Texas hotel. *The Grifters* was published in 1963, but it has the ambience of the 1940s and 1950s, when Raymond Chandler, whom Thompson much admired, was writing hard-boiled fiction. In the case of *The Grifters*, Thompson was writing of the "golden age of the grift," the 1950s, although the story is set in the present.[2]

Like his other novels, *The Grifters* is unrelenting in its bleak portrayal of human nature. It centers on Roy Dillon, who is seriously considering going off the grift in favor of a more stable sort of existence. But such an ordered kind of life is not in the cards for Roy; after all, Thompson's crooked characters seldom go straight.

Thompson died in 1977; after his death, his fiction became popular. When a wag heard that Thompson was dead, he retorted, "Smart career move." Thompson was always taken more seriously in Europe than the United States, and the movies made from his fiction have often been made by European directors: most notably, *The Grifters* was directed by an Englishman, Stephen Frears, who brought an outsider's eye to the Los Angeles locations.[3]

"Martin Scorsese, who was producing the film, asked me to direct it," Frears remembered. "I saw it as a story of the price of survival. To me, Jim Thompson gave Greek tragedy to the underclass."[4] *The Grifters* was adapted to the screen by another eminent crime writer, the late Donald Westlake, who wrote *The Hunter* under the pseudonym Richard Stark, a novel that was made into the widely acclaimed movie *Point Blank* (1967).

After running into difficulties with the British Board of Film Censors with such ice-cold, disturbing movies as *The Hit* (1984), about a police informant, Frears was pleased to be invited to the United States to make a picture. For Roy Dillon's home, the location team chose the Bryson Hotel, which goes back to Chandler's heyday. It still exists as a slightly tarnished temporary home to transients like Roy Dillon, people who have no roots. Lilly Dillon, his mother, comes to see him after having abandoned him eight years before. Now that he is an adult, Lilly flirts with him in a casual sort of way. Clearly Lilly is not your average mother, but at times she seems protective of her son. Frears comments, "*White Heat* touched on a similar situation: powerful familial feelings and mother love in a gangster context" (see chapter 5).

"While the plot of the film remains very close to the novel," Jane Haspel points out in *Novels into Film*, the "emphasis is less on Roy and more on Lilly Dillon's ability to survive."[5] Frears was glad to import cinematographer Oliver Stapleton from England to photograph the movie, but he was also pleased to have access in Hollywood to composer Elmer Bernstein (*The Sweet Smell of Success*, 1957), whose evocative film scores at times featured jazz motifs and other rhythms. The main theme he employs throughout *The Grifters* calls for brass and percussion, including the piano as a percussive instrument.

The film starts with a printed quotation from the lyrics of "The Lady Is a Tramp," by Lorenz Hart (with music by Richard Rodgers), with the word *grifted* underlined on the screen:

> I've wined and dined on Mulligan stew
> And never asked for turkey,
> As I hitched and hiked and *grifted* too
> From Maine to Albuquerque.

The movie proper begins at the Del Mar racetrack, with producer Martin Scorsese explaining the following over the sound track: "Around the country the bookies pay off winners at track odds. It's dangerous when a long shot comes in—unless you have someone at the track to lower the odds." That is precisely what Lilly Dillon does at Del Mar.

Lilly Dillon (Anjelica Huston), Roy Dillon (John Cusack), and Myra Langtry (Annette Bening), the three central characters, are first seen by the viewer in a split-screen triptych. Lilly is placing bets with Mafia money, ultimately to the benefit of Bobo Justus's Mafia mob. Meanwhile, Roy, who asks for change for a $20 bill, is caught trying to cheat a bartender out of $10; the bartender punches Roy in the stomach with a club in retaliation. In the meantime, Myra fails to pass off a phony necklace to a jeweler, who assumes (quite wrongly) that Myra was unaware that the jewels are worthless.

As the movie gets under way, Frears inserts a significant flashback of Roy in his teens. A traveling man in a bus station teaches Roy how to con a gullible mark (victim of a grift) in a card game. The stranger's parting advice is, "To con your partner, who knows you, that's a real score." The card sharp's lesson marks the beginning of Roy's career as a grifter, but Roy lacks the gumption to move beyond the petty grifting that his self-appointed mentor taught him.

When Lilly reenters Roy's life by going to see him at the Bryson Hotel, where he is staying, her maternal solicitude tells her that Roy is bleeding internally from the brutal whack in the stomach he sustained from the burly bartender. She takes him to a nearby hospital, where a doctor informs her that her son has an internal hemorrhage. Suddenly her maternal feelings for her son ignite, as she snaps at the doctor, "You know who I work for. My son is going to be alright; if not, I'll have you killed!" Roy says laconically to Lilly, "I guess I owe you my life." She answers, "You always did." She reminds him that she is his birth mother, even though she abandoned him when he was still a child. Lilly and Roy obviously have a love–hate relationship. Concerned for his welfare now that he is back in her life, she tells Roy, "Get off the grift, Roy. You're not tough enough for the rackets." Referring to his hospitalization, she adds, "You don't have the stomach for it." She realizes that, had she raised him, she would have made him tougher than he is.

When Myra and Lilly meet at Roy's hospital bedside, Myra realizes that if she wants to manipulate Roy into becoming her partner in a big con she has planned, she will have to eliminate the intrusive Lilly. Sweet-faced Myra, who is really an evil Kewpie doll, as one reviewer put it, is at present

Annette Bening and Anjelica Huston "comfort" John Cusack in *The Grifters* (1990).

in dire straits: she is reduced to having sex with her tubby landlord to pay the rent on her shabby apartment. She clearly needs a partner in crime.

At the Del Mar racetrack in La Jolla, Lilly meets her Mafia boss, Bobo Justus. The late, great Pat Hingle plays the corpulent Bobo; chomping on a cigar, he recalls Al Capone. An experienced gangster, Bobo has figured out that Lilly has been skimming off some of the profits of her racetrack con. Bobo takes her to his mansion; following the code of the Mafia, he punishes her by sadistically burning her hand with a lighted cigar to discourage her from cheating him again.

Myra persists in endeavoring to lure Roy into partnership with her in a big con. She reminisces about her previous cohort, Cole, saying with some admiration, "He was so crooked, he could eat soup with a corkscrew." When Roy continues to turn her down, she finally infers that Lilly and Roy harbor incestuous feelings, which apparently are mutual. "When Myra puts her finger on the oedipal source" of Roy's complicated relationship with Lilly, and on Roy's "violent rejection of her as a fellow con, their relationship collapses."[6]

Myra, fit to be tied, phones Bobo and informs him that Lilly continues to skim money from her racetrack con, money that belongs to Bobo; she even plots to murder Lilly. Learning that Myra has blown the whistle on her, Lilly is on the run, trying to escape Bobo and his gang. Myra tracks Lilly to a trashy back-road motel; she finds Lilly asleep and accordingly pounces on her, attempting to strangle her. The police discover a corpse in Lilly's bed and ask Roy to identify the body in the morgue. The corpse's face is disfigured, but he discovers that the deceased does not have a scar on her hand, which was the result of Bobo's burning Lilly's hand with a cigar. Roy realizes that the corpse is Myra, whom Lilly overpowered in her motel room and shot in the face to render Myra unrecognizable, but he identifies the body as Lilly anyway since he wants his mother declared legally dead to get Bobo off her trail. Such is Roy's filial concern for his mother.

Lilly goes to Roy's apartment in his absence and finds the money he has amassed from his various grifts. She discovers the loot behind a grotesque painting of a clown hanging on his wall and stuffs the cash into a suitcase. When Roy appears, she begs him to let her keep the loot because she needs ready cash to keep one step ahead of Bobo and his mob. Roy refuses her entreaties because he maintains that he needs the money to live on. Banking on Roy's attraction to her, Lilly desperately attempts to seduce him by saying that she is not really his mother, intimating that she can make love to him in exchange for his cash.

Roy sees through Lilly's ploy, and Lilly, at her wit's end, clouts him with the suitcase full of his money, just as he takes a glass of water. Lilly had intended to knock Roy out, but she accidentally smashes the water glass against his neck and cuts his throat with a jagged piece of glass. She sobs in anguish for all of a minute or two at the thought of having killed her son, but she regains enough of her composure to scoop up the money that has fluttered to the floor and stuff the bills, which have blood on them, back into the suitcase.

Lilly takes the elevator to the parking garage to take possession of Roy's car. Frears photographs Lilly through the iron grille on the elevator. He comments, "This is Lilly's descent into hell." Moreover, photographing Lilly through the elevator grille is apparently a homage to John Huston's *Maltese Falcon*, wherein the villainess is photographed by Huston through the elevator's iron grille to prefigure her going to prison for her crimes.

Raymond Chandler once said that one major character in a crime novel or film should have the chance for redemption, but in *The Grifters*, none of the main characters—Lilly, Roy, or Myra—are "redeemable."[7] For example, Roy realizes in the end that "his life of crime has poisoned every possible human relationship." And so, being faithful to Thompson's novel, *The Grifters* offers the "bleakest view of criminal society" of any gangster picture.[8]

When *The Grifters* was released, it made Stephen Frears a director of international renown. The movie was generally applauded; Richard Corliss calls the film a "gem—small, cold, bright, brilliantly crafted."[9] In contrast to the dark, brooding atmosphere of many gangster pictures, Frears moved his film into the sunshine of Los Angeles, and made the most successful adaptation of a Thompson novel ever filmed.

The Departed (2006)

Martin Scorsese wanted to make a movie about gangsters; still, he was not interested in small-time grifters, but organized crime. This is understandable because he was raised in a tenement in New York City's Little Italy, where the Mafia held sway. Even as a youngster, Scorsese felt that he could make a good gangster picture if he became a film director because he knew that world. It was a rough, primitive, savage world where organized crime was a way of life.

Scorsese aspired to become either a priest or a filmmaker. He did not last long in the seminary, but he went on to enroll in the film school at New York University, from which he graduated in 1964. As Les Keyser writes in his critical study of Scorsese, the budding director realized that "his Italian heritage, his Catholic faith, and his inner turmoil" about his personal problems "could all be synthesized onscreen."[10] Specifically, Scorsese wanted to "balance the values of family, Church, and tradition against the materialism, deception, and violence of the Mafia."[11]

The film that really launched Scorsese's career as a moviemaker was a low-budget, independent picture entitled *Mean Streets* (1973), which proved to be a substantial critical favorite. In it, Charlie (Harvey Keitel) attempts to reconcile his Catholic upbringing with his crime-ridden life as a Mafia hood. As Charlie muses quite seriously, "You don't fuck around with the Infinite." After his career took off, Scorsese made films in various genres, including three superior gangster movies: *Goodfellas* (1990); *Casino* (1995); and *The Departed* (2006), which was the best of the three.

The Departed is derived from a film made in Hong Kong in 2002, Wai Keung Lau and Siu Fai Mak's *Infernal Affairs*, in which an undercover cop infiltrates a gang and a deep-cover gangster joins the police force. "Scorsese is steeped in the movie past," says A. O. Scott.[12] Says Scorsese, "My father took me to see a double feature of *Little Caesar* and *The Public Enemy* in 1954, when I was a kid. I saw the rise and fall of a gangster; I never forgot that *Little Caesar* concludes with the fall of Rico, just as *The Public Enemy* ends with the death of Tom Powers. There is no happy ending" in either picture (see chapter 2).[13] So, too, Frank Costello, the Godfather, meets a grim fate in *The Departed*. By the same token, another classic gangster picture, *White Heat*, ties in with *The Departed*. In *White Heat*, Edmond O'Brien is an undercover cop (see chapter 5). Scorsese's version of *Infernal Affairs* is an improvement on the original Hong Kong movie, since his film clarifies the convoluted plot considerably; indeed, William Monaghan won an Academy Award for his screenplay for *The Departed*.

The cinematographer on *The Departed* was Michael Ballhaus, who was director of photography for Rainer Werner Fassbinder in Berlin for fifteen films before decamping for Hollywood and becoming Scorsese's favorite cameraman. Ballhaus's fluid camera work was perfectly in tune with the quick-fire cinematography Scorsese favored for *The Departed*.

The present film takes place in South Boston, known by the locals as "Southie," which is the stamping grounds of the Irish Mafia. Scorsese says that he had no trouble transplanting his knowledge of the Italian Mafia in Little Italy to the Irish Mafia in Southie. Francis (Frank) Costello (Jack Nicholson), the king of the Irish Mafia in Southie, was modeled on James "Whitey" Bulger, a notorious gangster who terrorized the residents of Southie for decades.

The Public Enemy, we recall, began with a gangster influencing Tom Powers to become a criminal when he grew up. So, too, *The Departed* begins with Colin Sullivan (Matt Damon), as a youngster, entering a grocery store, where Frank Costello is collecting protection money from the grocer. Costello immediately recognizes Colin as a kid who lives with his grandmother, and he orders the grocer to give him extra groceries to take home. Then Costello says to Colin, "If you want to earn some extra money, come and see me." He adds, "A man makes his own way. Nobody gives you anything; you have to take it." Costello is grooming the lad at this early age to grow up to be a member of his gang.

Scorsese cuts to Sullivan some years later, as a student at the police academy; when he graduates, he is inducted into the Special Investigation Unit (SIU), which deals with organized crime. The crisp, brisk editing of this montage of Sullivan going from being a lad in a grocery store to a graduate of the police academy exemplifies the adroit manner in which film editor Thelma Schoonmaker cut this film (and other Scorsese movies). It is small wonder that she won an Academy Award for her work on *The Departed*.

Sullivan warns the other members of the SIU that he has gathered evidence that Costello has a rat informant in the SIU (who happens to be Sullivan himself). Meanwhile, Billy Costigan (Leonardo DiCaprio), another student at the police academy, is persuaded by Captain Charles Queenan (Martin Sheen) and Sergeant Dignam (Mark Wahlberg) to become an undercover agent in Costello's gang. They arrange for him to have a short jail sentence for assault and battery to give credibility to his cover as a failed cop. When he gets out of jail, Queenan and Dignam place him on probation; they alone know he is undercover.

Scorsese provides love interest in the movie by having Sullivan and Costigan both fall in love with the same young woman—a police psychiatrist named Madolyn (Vera Formiga). She has a love relationship with Sullivan but is also having an affair with Costigan, who has to see her regularly as part of his probation program. Neither Sullivan nor Costigan knows of the other's involvement with Madolyn. For her part, Madolyn overlaps the worlds of Sullivan and Costigan.[14]

Madolyn, in due course, discovers that she is pregnant. She encourages Sullivan to claim paternity of the child, since, by this time, they are engaged to be married. She ultimately decides to give up her post as a police psychiatrist, having realized that she has gotten emotionally involved with two men she is supposed to be counseling.

Sullivan warns Costello that the SIU is going to raid his operation; of course, the raid is a dismal failure. Then Costigan tells Dignam that Costello knew about the raid in advance. He concludes, "There is a leak in the police department *from the inside.*" Dignam concurs: "The police department has more leaks than the Iraqi Navy."

To identify the police rat working for Costello, Costigan follows Costello to a secret meeting with the rat informant in an adult movie theater. Costello meets Sullivan there, while Costigan watches them from a back row. Costello gives Sullivan an envelope containing information about his gang that may help Sullivan identify the police informant in his mob (who is Costigan). Scorsese demonstrates his total control of his material in the next sequence: Costigan cannot make out Sullivan's face in the dark theater, so he follows Sullivan when he walks out of the establishment. Sullivan's figure, however, is obscured as he walks down the shadowy streets; moreover, there is steam coming up from the vents along the way that clouds Costigan's vision as he attempts to shadow Sullivan. This is an example of the masterful way in which Scorsese, in tandem with his cinematographer, lit this location. Costigan finally follows Sullivan down a murky alley but loses him.

Sullivan subsequently has some dirty cops tail Queenan when he goes to a clandestine meeting on the rooftop of a vacant building with his police informant in Costello's gang. Costigan avoids detection, and Sullivan's gang takes out on Queenan their consternation at allowing the police rat informant to get away by pitching Queenan off the roof. When Dignam, back at headquarters, learns of Queenan's murder, he

Leonardo DiCaprio and Jack Nicholson in *The Departed* (2006).

goes berserk and attacks Sullivan, whom he does not trust. Dignam is accordingly suspended from the force. Thus, Costigan has lost the only two contacts he had on the police force.

Sullivan participates in a raid on Costello's warehouse, where Costello is planning to close an illicit international sale of weaponry to Chinese buyers, whom Costello refers to as "Bruce Lee and the Karate Kids." Scorsese stages this meeting as a superb set piece in the picture. Sullivan takes Costello aside and tells him that he has reason to believe that Costello has informed on one of his own mob to the FBI to keep from being busted for some of his crimes. Costello replies that he has occasionally found it advantageous to feed information to the feds, but he swears that he has never ratted on Sullivan, because, he says, "you are like a son to me." Costello's lugubrious response does not mollify Sullivan, who is shocked that even Costello is a rat police informant. In a rage, Sullivan fires several bullets into his erstwhile father figure.

Soon thereafter, Costigan pays a visit to the police station and notices on Sullivan's desk the envelope that Costello had given his police informant at the porno theater. Costigan finds some tapes of furtive phone conversations between Sullivan and Costello that were hidden in Costello's office. He ships them to Sullivan's apartment. Because Madolyn is still cohabiting with Sullivan, she intercepts the package when it arrives and opens it. She listens to one of the incriminating tapes. Despite Sullivan's attempt to explain away his relationship with Costello, Madolyn walks out on him in a fit of rage.

Costigan demands that Sullivan meet with him on the same rooftop where Queenan was killed. He confronts Sullivan and arrests him for betraying the SIU. But Costigan is murdered on the spot by Barrigan (James Badge Dale), yet another of Costello's informants on the police force. Thinking fast, Sullivan shoots Barrigan dead and later testifies that Barrigan alone was Costello's police informant. He recommends Costigan for a posthumous medal of merit; Sullivan attends Costigan's funeral, which is a full-dress affair, complete with twenty-one-gun salute. Sullivan waits for Madolyn after the burial service, but the gaunt, determined Madolyn, staring impassively ahead, walks toward the camera, past Sullivan, and out of the cemetery. Scorsese lifted this shot from the final scene of Carol Reed's *The Third Man* (1949).

In the last scene of the present film, Sullivan enters his apartment, where he finds Dignam waiting for him. Dignam blows away Sullivan, whom he figured out was a rat informant for Costello in the police department. By killing Sullivan, Dignam has taken the law into his own hands, just as Eliot Ness did when he killed Frank Nitti in *The Untouchables* (see chapter 10). After Dignam leaves, the camera glides past the corpse of Sullivan, who is now one of the departed, to the living room window, where a rat is scurrying across the windowsill, symbolizing that Sullivan, despite his surface charm, was fundamentally a rat. Through Sullivan's living room window, the State House is visible across the street. The State House, with its golden dome dazzling in the sunlight, represents Sullivan's aspirations to become a decent, law-abiding police detective, an aspiration he never fulfilled.

Whitey Bulger, the model for the character of Frank Costello, was still at large when *The Departed* was released; he had taken off for parts unknown. Recent reports declare that the FBI caught up with him, and he finally went to trial for his crimes in June 2013. His defense was so convoluted and confusing that it is unlikely that he will be acquitted.[15]

When I spoke with Martin Scorsese while he was making a film on location in New York, I asked him for his approach to violence on the screen. He answered, "I do not glamorize violence in my movies, nor is the violence gratuitous. I put violence on the screen in the way I see it."[16] The Academy of Motion Picture Arts and Sciences conferred an Oscar on Scorsese as Best Director for *The Departed*; the picture also received the Oscar for Best Picture, as well as Academy Awards for Best Screenplay and Best Editing, as mentioned earlier. Rarely has a gangster picture been so honored by the Academy.

In the *Film Guide*, Leslie Halliwell states that the picture is "well worth the plaudits" and has "some superbly staged set pieces"; for example, Costigan tailing Sullivan through the sinister streets and alleys of Southie. David Ansen praises the film in *Newsweek* but cautions that it is "not for the faint of heart." Tom Charity of CNN calls it a "model of smooth precision."[17] Leonard Matlin terms *The Departed* a "potent, violent yarn" with "vibrant performances."[18] Gerald Mast and Bruce Kawin's film history describes the picture as reaching deep levels of "darkness and betrayal" that reveal the "absolute stylistic control and enormous range of the films of Scorsese's maturity."[19] In short, *The Departed* is arguably Scorsese's masterpiece.

CHAPTER TWELVE
DILLINGER AND PUBLIC ENEMIES

Dillinger (1945)

The first motion picture made about John Dillinger was Max Nosseck's *Dillinger* (1945), and the most recent one was Michael Mann's *Public Enemies* (2009). In between these two films there have been others, for example, John Milius's *Dillinger* (1973), but the Nosseck and Mann movies are the two Dillinger pictures that are most worthy of discussion.

Max Nosseck made the first Dillinger film at Monogram Studios in 1945. Monogram was one of the minor studios on Hollywood's "Poverty Row," also known as "Gower Gulch," since some of these small-time studios were located on Gower Street. Monogram was notable as the studio where the Dead End Kids (now known as the East Side Kids) wound up after they left Warner Bros. in 1938.

Joseph Breen, the industry censor, had squelched the trigger-happy gangster cycle of the 1930s in a directive dated July 15, 1935, by warning that he would reject any movie inspired by the life of John Dillinger or any other notable criminal. Screenwriter Philip Yordan, who wrote the script for *Dillinger*, stated that the "majors agreed not to make a picture about Dillinger because of the pressure from the censorship office, but Monogram was not a major studio." It did not belong to the Motion Picture Association of America and did not endorse the agreement made by the majors.[1] And so they produced *Dillinger*.

John Dillinger was born in Indiana, in 1902, "into a strict religious family, against which he rebelled early on." He committed his first robbery at the age of twenty-one; inexplicably, the judge threw the book at him, giving him a ten-year sentence, although he was a first-time offender. He was paroled in 1933. He commented at the time that the state had stolen ten years of his life, adding, "now I'm going to do some stealing of my own." His lawless career primarily consisted of ten bank robberies, but he was mythologized by the public as an American Robin Hood, who only stole from the rich; that is, the hated banks that had foreclosed on their homes and farms during the Depression, which had just ended.[2] Yordan's screenplay, at Breen's behest, avoided presenting Dillinger as a champion of the dispossessed. His fast-paced screenplay portrays Dillinger as a violent, brutal sociopath. A hooker named Anna Sage finally put the finger on Dillinger; an FBI squad led by Agent Melvin Purvis shot him down in July 1934.

Yordan's screenplay contains as much fiction as fact. There is no mention that Agent Purvis was responsible for Dillinger's demise, nor is Anna Sage, the brothel keeper who tipped off Purvis, mentioned. Instead, the female who turns Dillinger in to the FBI is called Helen Rodgers. She blows the whistle on Dillinger because she has gotten cabin fever from hiding out with him in a dingy Chicago apartment. In any event, Breen's office approved Yordan's script, with few alterations.

Dillinger was produced by the King Brothers, Maurice and Frank. They had begun their careers as bootleggers and graduated into producing low-budget program pictures; they became known for their crime pictures. Monogram budgeted *Dillinger* at less than $50,000, which was small change in Hollywood. The King Brothers hired Max Nosseck to direct the picture. He was born in Poland and had directed a number of films, mostly in Berlin, until he was forced to flee Europe after the Nazis came to power. He eventually settled in Hollywood, where he directed movies on Poverty Row.

Lawrence Tierney, a native of Brooklyn, was picked to play Dillinger partly because he hung around the King Brothers' office, and he looked to them like a thug. According to Yordan, Tierney was paid $375 for three weeks' work. Admittedly, he lacked experience, and Nosseck frequently hollered at him on the set during rehearsals. Actor Marc Lawrence (*Key Largo* and *The Asphalt Jungle*) remembered Nosseck, who was slightly more than five feet tall, blustering at Tierney one day and calling him stupid. "Tierney came alive." He shouted back at Nosseck, "Say that again, you son of a bitch!" Lawrence explained, "For the first time in the whole picture he was a terror. Little Max's screaming brought him out of his shell."[3] It is surprising that the Brothers King were able to engage veteran composer Dimitri Tiomkin to score a second feature at Monogram, because he had already earned his spurs writing the music for Hitchcock's *Shadow of a Doubt* (1943) and other major motion pictures.

Nosseck brought the film in on budget and on schedule, probably because he interpolated stock footage from earlier gangster movies into *Dillinger*. The stock footage accounted for a third of the movie's seventy-minute running time. The most noteworthy scene extracted from an earlier gangster picture was the armored truck robbery from Fritz Lang's *You Only Live Once* (see chapter 8).[4]

Dillinger opens with a prologue in which Dillinger's father (Victor Kilian) comes onstage in a movie theater after a newsreel about his son John has been shown and addresses the audience about his late son's

Lawrence Tierney in *Dillinger* (1945).

criminal career. Mr. Dillinger did, in fact, tour movie theaters in various cities after his son's death, presumably because he needed the money paid to him by the exhibitors. He appears onstage rather timidly, hat in hand. "John grew up like other country boys in Indiana," he begins. "But he got tired of doing routine jobs; one day he left home to find a job in the big city," Indianapolis. The film then tells the story of John Dillinger in flashback.

Dillinger is discovered in a seedy bar with a peroxide blonde, who wants another high ball. He is fresh out of cash, and when the waiter refuses to allow him to put the drinks on a tab, he goes to a nearby grocery store, robs it of $20, and pays the bill. But he is soon caught and jailed.

His cell mate is "Specs" Green, played by Edmund Lowe (*Dinner at Eight*), whom Dillinger respects because he masterminded a bank robbery that netted him $70,000—a sum far exceeding the paltry amount Dillinger got for his grocery stickup. Dillinger promises to spring Specs and two other inmates, Doc Madison (Marc Lawrence) and Kirk Otto, played by Elisha Cook Jr. (*The Maltese Falcon*), from prison after he gets out. Dillinger makes good his promise by smuggling rifles into the jail for his buddies after he is released. John Milius, who directed the 1973 *Dillinger*, comments, "I like the cut from the shot of the guys receiving the guns [that] Dillinger sent them to the shot of them robbing a bank with the same guns."[5] In a movie with the jejune running time of seventy minutes, speedy editing of this sort is essential.

Dillinger returns to the tawdry bar to revenge himself on the waiter who embarrassed him in front of his girl. "The killing is the most creative scene in the film, as the waiter is mauled by Dillinger with the jagged edge of a broken beer mug," Marilyn Yaquinto observes. "At the moment of the assault, which occurs off-camera, the piano player is shown frantically banging on the keys to match the violent act."[6] Much of the violence takes place offscreen, as in this scene, because the King Brothers wanted to ward off complaints from Breen that the movie contains too much bloody violence.

The next heist involves robbing an armored truck carrying payroll money. (The footage is from Lang's *You Only Live Once*.) After the successful heist, Dillinger ousts Specs as leader of the gang and replaces him because he is convinced that Specs is getting too old to be in charge. The gang holes up in the Little Bohemia Lodge, in Wisconsin, between bank robberies, which they commit in neighboring states.

Dillinger is captured by the police and jailed in an Indiana prison; he smugly tells the press, "No tank town jail can hold me." He covertly sets out whittling a gun out of a hunk of wood, which he blackens with shoe polish. Then—true to his word—he breaks out of prison, with his fake gun.

Back at the Little Bohemia Lodge, he catches the elderly couple who run the lodge surreptitiously endeavoring to place a phone call to the police to give the gang away. He foils their attempt and shoots them both. Helen Rogers (Anne Jeffreys), his present gun moll, is appalled by the double murder. This fictitious incident serves to undercut any sympathy the viewer might have for Dillinger, who is, after all, no Robin Hood. The FBI raids the lodge; Dillinger gets away, but his gang members give themselves up. Doc Madison and the others were aware that their funds were running low, and, with the Feds closing in, it seemed the wisest course.

Dillinger and Rogers are hiding out in a Chicago rooming house. Rogers grows bored hanging around a furnished room for weeks on end, waiting for the "big heat" to cool down. Dillinger decides that they should take in a movie, and Helen takes the opportunity to tip off the Feds. She tells them that she will wear a red dress so that they can easily spot her with Dillinger, hence she became known in folklore as the "lady in red." Actually, the press said that she was wearing a red dress because red has always been associated with a "scarlet woman," which Helen certainly was.

They attend the Biograph Theater to see *Manhattan Melodrama*, with Clark Gable as a gangster somewhat modeled on Dillinger. As they leave the theater, Helen pulls away from Dillinger, and he sees the FBI agents. He shoots it out with them in the alley next to the theater, and Dillinger is killed. "People dipped their handkerchiefs in his blood, as if he were a holy icon," says Milius. Obviously this does not happen in the film. "He ends his life in an alley, betrayed by the woman that he loved," concludes Milius, except that Dillinger did not love the "woman in red"; his beloved was Billie Frechette, who appears in *Public Enemies*. She was in prison when Dillinger was shot, as we shall see later in this chapter.

"Breen's office passed the film with very little problem." After all, the movie "gave the audience a classic example of how crime doesn't pay," just as Breen had stipulated that it should.[7] *Variety*, the show business Bible, gave *Dillinger* a positive review, saying that, "Lawrence Tierney stood out," in spite of the fact that "Joe Breen's boys clamped down on the script."[8] Similarly, the *Hollywood Reporter* declares that *Dillinger* "recalls the vigor and excitement of the gangster film cycle."[9] This is understandable, since the movie contains clips from some of the 1930s gangster movies.

Nosseck continued to direct low-budget programmers in Hollywood; for instance, *Black Beauty* (1946), about a beloved horse. He returned to Germany in the late 1950s and continued to make films. Like Robert Siodmak (*Criss Cross*), he ended his film career where he had begun it. Lawrence Tierney achieved instant fame with *Dillinger*, but he still had to travel a bumpy road in Hollywood. Like Sterling Hayden (*The Asphalt Jungle*), Tierney was uncooperative and difficult for directors to work with. Moreover, he was a heavy drinker and was frequently arrested for drunken and disorderly conduct, so he seldom got plum roles. But he did play a psychotic killer opposite Claire Trevor (*Key Largo*) in Robert Wise's *Born to Kill* (1947). Philip Yordan received an Oscar nomination for his screenplay for *Dillinger*. Suffice it to say Academy Award nominations for Monogram pictures were few and far between.

John Milius, as noted, made another *Dillinger* in 1973, a good but unremarkable picture. Then Michael Mann decided to make his own Dillinger movie, entitled *Public Enemies* (2009); the plural title is apparently meant to suggest that the picture not only covers John Dillinger, but also Baby Face Nelson, who, for a time, belonged to his gang, and also Pretty Boy Floyd, whom Melvin Purvis defeated before he got around to Dillinger. At all events, even in 2009, Tierney's *Dillinger* of 1945 remains the Dillinger picture to beat.

Public Enemies (2009)

Michael Mann had become familiar with the gangster genre working on the television series *Miami Vice* in the 1980s. He made the first movie about the psychotic psychiatrist Hannibal Lecter, called *Manhunter* (1981), which later became a franchise under other directors (*The Silence of the Lambs*, etc.). He continued focusing on the cat-and-mouse game of police pursuit with *Heat* (1995), costarring Al Pacino (*The Godfather: Part II*) and Robert De Niro (*The Untouchables*).[10]

Dante Spinotti, the Italian cinematographer, has often worked in Hollywood and has brought his superior craftsmanship to Mann's *Manhunter*, *Heat*, and *Public Enemies*. Johnny Depp, who plays John Dillinger in *Public Enemies*, also appeared in the Mafia film *Donnie Brasco* (1998). Christian Bale, who costars with Depp as FBI agent Melvin Purvis, is versatile enough to play heroes like Purvis and such villains as the title role in *American Psycho* (2000).

Mann's film is adapted from Bryan Burrough's book *Public Enemies*; the movie tries to hew close to the facts as presented by Burrough, and hence present a more authentic version of Dillinger's life than Max Nosseck did in *Dillinger*.[11] The present picture begins with a brief printed prologue: "1933: It's the fourth year of the Depression. For John Dillinger, Alvin Karpis, and Baby Face Nelson, it is the glorious age of bank robbery."

The movie proper begins with Dillinger engineering a jail break of some inmate friends of his a mere eight weeks after he himself was paroled. He says to them, as their getaway car speeds away from the Indiana State Prison in Michigan City, "Let's go to Chicago and make some money." The camera cuts to Melvin Purvis, engaged in a gun battle with Pretty Boy Floyd (Channing Tatum) in an orchard in the wilderness. Purvis shoots Floyd dead with a rifle and is lauded by the press as a true gangbuster.

During a news conference, J. Edgar Hoover (Billy Crudup) announces that he has appointed Purvis bureau chief of the FBI in Chicago, with a mandate to bring John Dillinger to justice. Chicago, emphasizes Hoover, is the center of the crime wave that is sweeping across the United States. John Dillinger is the first criminal to be named public enemy number one by Hoover.

Public Enemies is twice the length of the 1945 *Dillinger*, partly because Mann, unlike Nosseck, focuses on Dillinger's romance with Billie Frechette, played by Oscar-winning actress Marion Cotillard (*La Viern Rose*). When Dillinger makes a play for Billie in a Chicago nightclub, she confesses that her mother was a native—American: "Most men don't like that." Dillinger, who could be a gentleman when he cared to, responds, "I am not most men." Billie is not a blushing rose: she is not abashed that this nightclub is frequented by the likes of Dillinger, Alvin Karpis (Giovanni Ribisi), and Frank Nitti (Bill Camp), Capone's right-hand man, who was erroneously depicted as being killed by Eliot Ness in *The Untouchables* (see chapter 10). Dillinger takes one look at Nitti and observes, "He looks like a barber," meaning an Italian. In his conversation with Karpis, Alvin tells Dillinger that he must plan ahead and not just live for the moment; Dillinger unwisely disagrees. That is Dillinger's crucial mistake: by film's end he is bereft of the resources and manpower to continue his lawless career.

Dillinger was brought up to be a well-mannered person and, as such, was liked by reporters and the public. "Most people blamed the banks for the Depression," Mann explains. "A lot of ordinary people blamed the government for not being able to cope with the problems of the poor and homeless."[12] Like Bonnie and Clyde, Dillinger always maintained that he was robbing the rich (the banks) and not the poor and disenfranchised. Consequently, as a rule, the public and press would not betray him to the authorities; as mentioned, they thought that that would be like betraying Robin Hood.[13] A member of Dillinger's gang quips at one point, "The whole country thinks you're a goddamn hero!"

Johnny Depp as John Dillinger in *Public Enemies* (2009).

There is one scene in *Public Enemies* that did not actually take place. In reality, the head of the Indiana State Police came to see Dillinger in jail. That inspired Mann to employ some dramatic license and have Melvin Purvis pay a visit to Dillinger in prison, since they were the two "mighty opposites" in conflict (to borrow a phrase from John Milton). Mann notes, "They are like two fighters getting in the ring, trying to figure how to knock each other out." (Mann is recalling his boxing movie *Ali*.) Dillinger greets Purvis in the scene as the "man who killed Pretty Boy Floyd." Purvis declares stoically, as he leaves, "The only way you're going to leave this jail cell is when we execute you."

But Dillinger does, in fact, escape from jail with the help of a fake gun, as already discussed. He then steals a bona fide gun from the prison arsenal and takes off in Sheriff Lillian Holley's (Lili Taylor) own automobile. He drives past the prison guards at the front gate because they assume that Sheriff Holley is behind the wheel. When Dillinger gets back to Chicago, he seeks asylum with a crony who now runs a money laundering business for the Syndicate; he informs Dillinger that he can no longer afford to harbor "celebrity gangsters" like Dillinger.

"After Prohibition, bootleggers gradually moved into organized crime," Mann comments. "Dillinger is a nineteenth-century bandit, like Jesse James. He is an anachronism in the world of organized crime. He remains an independent gangster with a mob of his own. After a bank robbery, he and his outfit hole up in the Little Bohemia Lodge, a roadhouse in upstate Wisconsin. As a matter of fact, Dillinger has been forced to replace members of the gang who have been killed or jailed with men that he sees as inferior to them. For example, Baby Face Nelson has joined Dillinger's mob. At the outset of one bank robbery, Nelson hoists himself up on a table and recklessly waves his tommy gun at the bank guards. Nelson is not as professional or disciplined as Dillinger's previous gang members.

Meanwhile, Hoover is increasingly frantic that Purvis has not taken down Dillinger in the way that he nailed Pretty Boy Floyd. He fears that the bureau is becoming the laughing stock of the entire nation, particularly after Dillinger escaped prison with a toy gun. Hoover orders Purvis to arrest Dillinger's known associates, including his relatives. Bryan Burrough comments that, "Hoover believed in playing rough with people who knew Dillinger," while Purvis was more and more convinced that

"Hoover was not an honorable man."[14] Nevertheless, Hoover was his boss, and Purvis did what he was told.

Hoover encourages Purvis to employ torture during interrogations if need be. In a subsequent scene, a cohort of Dillinger's, who was wounded in an exchange of gunfire with the feds, is being interrogated by an agent while he is in the hospital, in Purvis's presence. The man screams for some pain killers, which the attending physician wants to give him. Purvis replies, "When you tell us what we want to know." Then Purvis tells the doctor, "If you interfere, I will arrest you."

The patient finally divulges that the Dillinger gang is at the Little Bohemia Lodge. He then spits in the face of the agent interrogating him. Purvis takes a passel of agents to the lodge, and they open fire on the rooms occupied by Dillinger and his mob. Dillinger, however, adroitly escapes through a back window and gets away. This scene was shot where it happened, at the lodge; the bullet holes in the lodge walls, which are relics of this gun battle, are still there. Dillinger speeds to Billie Frechette's apartment in Chicago and arrives just in time to see her being arrested by federal agents.

An FBI agent, following Hoover's orders, brutally beats Billie in an effort to make her reveal what she knows about Dillinger. When she passes out, Purvis intervenes and personally carries Billie out of the interrogation room, thereby indicating his misgivings about allowing his agents to use cruel tactics on suspects, particularly females.

Anna Sage, an illegal alien who runs the Chicago brothel where Dillinger is hiding out, contacts the bureau and tells Purvis that she will set a trap for Dillinger, provided that she is not deported back to her native Romania. A few days later, Anna phones Purvis and informs him that she and Dillinger are going to a movie at the Biograph Theater that night (July 22, 1934). Purvis has inferred that the money from Dillinger's bank robberies has dwindled to a pittance, and he is restless from living in a cramped room in a bordello. Thus, he is desperate for some relaxation. *Manhattan Melodrama*, with Clark Gable, is showing at the Biograph.

Public Enemies is the only Dillinger movie in which the real Biograph, at 2433 N. Lincoln Avenue, on Chicago's Near North Side, was actually used to stage Dillinger's final hours. Dillinger had recently undergone plastic surgery and had sprouted a moustache to alter his appearance, so

Anna told Purvis she would wear an orange skirt (*not* red, as the press stated) so the feds would recognize her.

Purvis and his squad wait for Dillinger to emerge from the Biograph Theater. When Purvis catches sight of Anna's orange skirt, he lights a cigar, which is the signal for his squad to draw their weapons. When Dillinger notices this, he quickly draws his own gun and runs into the alley next to the Biograph, which leads to Anna's place, his hangout. Agent Charles Winstead (Stephen Lang) fires the bullet that pierces Dillinger's brain. Anna disappears; Hoover subsequently overruled Purvis's promise to allow Anna to remain in the United States and has her shipped back to Romania. Winstead visits Billie Frechette in jail and tells her that Dillinger whispered in his ear as he died. Although what Dillinger said was not clear to Winstead, he reassured Billie that her lover's last thoughts were of her. It is this scene in which Cotillard is superb as Billie, as one critic later said. The film ends with a printed epilogue: "Melvin Purvis quit the FBI a year later and died by his own hand in 1960. Billie Frechette was released in 1936 and lived the rest of her life in Wisconsin."

Michael Mann observes that, "Melvin Purvis, as a Southern gentleman, had traditional values, such as chivalry. He did not approve of what Hoover made him do to defeat Dillinger." Christian Bale, who interviewed Melvin Purvis's son Alston, states, "By the time he got Dillinger, Melvin Purvis had compromised his values."[15] Hoover wanted to sweep under the rug Purvis's exploits in capturing gangsters, particularly public enemy number one, because Hoover was jealous of the adulation Purvis received as a result of the Dillinger case. He was determined that there would only be one famous person in the FBI: J. Edgar Hoover. Hoover gave Purvis a desk job during his last year with the bureau. He was apoplectic when Purvis wrote his autobiography, *An American Agent*, telling his side of the story.[16] "Much of Purvis's personal history was erased from the FBI files," Bale continues, "so that when I interviewed FBI agents about him, I told them more than they told me."[17]

Public Enemies was well received when it was released in 2009. Leonard Maltin calls it an "ambitious examination of famed Depression-era bank robber John Dillinger," saying it is "stylistically made, as expected from director, cowriter Mann. Marion Cotillard shines as Dillinger's girlfriend Billie Frechette."[18]

There has been an ongoing debate about the relative merits of the 1945 *Dillinger* and *Public Enemies*. Undoubtedly, *Public Enemies*, being a mainstream commercial Hollywood feature, possesses a professional polish lacking in the earlier low-budget programmer. Thus, in the original picture, the plot goes into overdrive before the moviegoer has the chance to get acquainted with the principals to the degree that one can in the later movie.

Because the first *Dillinger* film was made on the cheap and on the double, a couple of howlers were overlooked by the director. For example, the FBI agents are shown lined up outside the Biograph in the last scene, each with a tommy gun visible in his hand. They did not give themselves away in this fashion, because they would have precipitated a shootout in front of the theater and innocent bystanders would have been hit by stray bullets. The shootout took place, as we know, in the alley next to the theater.

Because *Public Enemies* is less tightly constructed than the first film, it contains a few slow-paced stretches that cause the viewer's interest to wane temporarily—something that never happens in the original film. In sum whether one believes that Nosseck's *Dillinger* is better than Mann's *Public Enemies* largely depends on whether one prefers fast-paced action movies, with a minimum of character development, to longer, somewhat slower—but denser—films that reflect a thorough analysis of the psychology of character. In the last analysis, both movies are worth seeing. As for Michael Mann, he remains "one of the most sought-after directors working in Hollywood today."[19] He continues to divide his time between features and working in TV.

GANGSTER SQUAD AND OTHER FILMS
Time Marches On and So Does
the Gangster Genre

When I was a youngster, the main feature at our local movie theater was often accompanied by a documentary short from the *March of Time* series. At the end of each of these documentary shorts, the narrator declares, "Time marches on!" And so, in this afterword, I repeat that "time marches on." In this instance, I refer to the fact that the gangster genre is now more than a century old. The genre began with the first officially recognized gangster pictures, D. W. Griffith's *The Muskateers of Pig Alley* and Josef von Sternberg's *Underworld*, and it has continued in popularity ever since.

Of course, gangster films include violence as an important ingredient, but then "violence has always been a part of entertainment," points out Martin Kaplan, director of the Norman Lear Center for the study of entertainment and society at the University of Southern California. "Violence is both a moneymaker—audiences love it—and an artist's tool." But it should never be allowed to overwhelm the human drama, nor should it be gratuitous. "For every Scorsese," Kaplan continues, "there is a schlockmeister" who invests in a movie with lots of violence just to sell more tickets.[1]

"Perhaps the gangster keeps drawing us to the movies," Marilyn Yaquinto hazards, because we see him as a nightmare version of "our own ambitions run amuck." Martin Scorsese perhaps best sums up the permanence of the gangster's character for us. Both *Mean Streets* (1973) and *The Departed* (2006)—which Scorsese made three decades apart—are about gangsters living a violent street life, marked by ferocity and a kind of camaraderie. This shows that "not much has changed" about the gangster genre after all. The characters in both *Mean Streets* and *The Departed* share the same depravity and commit similar gruesome crimes "on the same grimy streets that are fated always to be mean."[2]

In sum, the gangster genre continues to flourish. Foster Hirsch points out that in *The Departed*, "Scorsese uses an explosive syntax of quick cuts . . . a darting, hyperactive camera" to convey the corrupt world his characters inhabit.[3] Yet, the world of the gangster film is not as simple as it once was. In the gangster pictures of the 1930s, it was a world where "might makes right," and good guys and bad guys were easy to tell apart. In the later gangster movies treated in this book like *The Untouchables*, Eliot Ness learns that one must fight violence with violence. As a tough Irish cop instructs Ness, "To beat the Mob, shoot first and shoot fast." Such gangster films of the last twenty-five years as the *Godfather* trilogy, *The Untouchables*, and *The Departed* reflect "concerns about violence, ethnic conflicts, and moral values" more so than in the past.[4]

In *The Departed*, for example, the distinction between good cop/bad cop becomes blurred. Indeed, in both *The Untouchables* and *The Departed*, a law enforcement officer takes the law into his own hands to see that justice is done. Some critics complained that this seemed more like the law of the Wild West than the law of a civilized society. Despite such moral compromises, Hirsch writes, these movies "ultimately condemn the gangster's zealous pursuit of power and money"—as is the case with Al Capone in *The Untouchables* and Frank Costello in *The Departed*.[5]

Chinatown (1974)

This brings us to *Chinatown*, which I wanted to bring into relief at this point in this book. *Chinatown* is a period gangster film in which the hero runs afoul of the Syndicate in Los Angeles in the 1930s, the heyday of the gangster film cycle. The movie is based on an original screenplay by Robert Towne, who was known as an eminent script doctor in Hollywood, polishing the screenplays for such films as *The Godfather*. He offered the screenplay of *Chinatown* to Robert Evans, studio chief at Paramount, and Evans signed Jack Nicholson to play the lead. Nicholson, in turn, got Roman Polanski to agree to direct the movie.

Roman Polanski spent his childhood in the wretched Polish ghetto in Cracow during World War II. He later attended the Polish Film School and started his film career in Poland. Later he moved on to Hollywood, where he made the highly successful horror film *Rosemary's Baby* (1968).[6]

Although *Chinatown* is set in Los Angeles during the late 1930s, there was little doubt that a European could make an authentic film about Los Angeles. Foreign filmmakers, precisely because they are not American born, are able to view the culture and customs of a given country with a perceptive eye for the sort of telling details that homegrown directors might take for granted or simply overlook. As Alfred Hitchcock once said, the United States is mostly made up of foreigners.

Charles R. Berg describes the central character of a Robert Towne script as an "outsider living on the fringe . . . of an uncaring world."[7] That description typifies private investigator J. J. "Jake" Gittes (Jack Nicholson) in *Chinatown*, with his fumbling attempts to protect Evelyn Mulwray (Faye Dunaway) from her corrupt father, power broker and crime czar Noah Cross. Cross is something like Al Capone in the manner in which he runs a criminal organization. For Polanski, who grew up in occupied Poland, movie heroes are characters for whom a neat dramatic resolution is not a possibility. "Bob Towne wanted a happy ending," Polanski remembers. "He wanted Evelyn to survive and Cross to suffer for his crimes. I said that she must die if the film is to have any kind of meaning. I wrote the final scene a couple of nights before we shot it."[8]

"The title of the film," Towne explains, "came from a L.A. vice cop I knew." He once said to Towne, "When you are down in Chinatown, with the tongues and the different dialects, you can't tell who is doing what to whom." That is the problem that faces J. J. Gittes, private eye.

The director of photography on the picture was John Alonzo, who divided his time between feature films and television. His work in television had taught him to work quickly, which helped to keep the film on schedule. At the beginning of the film, Gittes is interviewing a client who identifies herself as Evelyn Mulwray. She wants him to follow her husband, Hollis Mulwray (Darrell Zwerling), the chief engineer of the Los Angeles Department of Water and Power, who is allegedly cheating on her. Gittes shadows Mulwray to a public hearing at the county courthouse, where a politician is giving a ferverino about Los Angeles needing another dam because the city sits on the edge of a desert. Hollis Mulwray insists that the proposed dam would inevitably collapse. Gittes also follows Mulwray to meet a young woman at the Almacondo Apartments.

Jack Nicholson and Faye Dunaway in *Chinatown* (1974).

Gittes is nonplussed when he has a visit from the real Evelyn Mulwray and realizes that he has been duped into following her husband for some unspecified reason. Towne comments that since Evelyn's name marks her as a daughter of Eve, a duplicitous figure in the Bible, the viewer assumes she is a femme fatale, but she is really the heroine of the movie, who works out of decent motives.

Gittes visits the reservoir where the drowned corpse of Hollis Mulwray is discovered. He encounters a pint-sized gangster known as the Midget (Roman Polanski), who accuses Gittes of being "nosy" and accordingly slits his nose with a switchblade. This abrupt eruption of violence signals that Gittes is in for more trouble. The gangster's white suit belies his dark character, since white usually symbolizes a spotless personality in a movie.

Gittes has a confrontation with Noah Cross, Evelyn's father, played by the great director John Huston (*The Maltese Falcon*) with a manner that Pauline Kael describes as "rotting charm."[9] Cross explains that he looks respectable because he is old: "Politicians, ugly buildings, and whores all look respectable if they last long enough." Cross is known to have several police officers and politicians in his pocket.

When talking with Gittes, Cross does not deny that Gittes was used as a cat's paw in the conspiracy to destroy Mulwray, Cross's former partner, by having Gittes hired by the spurious Evelyn Mulwray to shadow Mulwray. He warns Gittes not to believe anything his daughter tells him because "she is a disturbed woman." Cross offers Gittes a handsome retainer to "find the girl" that Gittes saw Hollis Mulwray conversing with at the Almacondo Apartments. The girl, Cross implies, is Mulwray's underage inamorata. His parting shot at Gittes is another warning: "You may think that you know what you are dealing with, but, believe me, you don't." After visiting the County Hall of Records, Gittes is convinced that Noah Cross is conning the city of Los Angeles into building a dam, but the water is not going to L.A.; it is going to the land in the valley that Cross secretly owns. This land will be invaluable once it has a steady water supply. Hollis Mulwray discovered Cross's plan to defraud the city of a fortune and was killed for it.[10]

Gittes pressures Evelyn Mulwray into admitting that the girl Gittes saw Hollis with is her sister and daughter. Katherine Cross is the result of a sexual encounter between Noah Cross and his daughter Evelyn. Her father is a maniacal power broker who is determined to control the future of Los Angeles.

Gittes convenes a meeting with Evelyn, Noah, and Katherine Cross in a shadowy area of Chinatown. At one point, Gittes inquires privately how Cross could have committed incest with his daughter. Cross, a died-in-the-wool sociopath, responds, "Most people need never have to find out that at the right time and in the right place they are capable of anything." Gittes urges Evelyn to turn her father over to the police, but she replies bitterly, "He *owns* the police!"

Because Evelyn is aware that Noah has designs on Katherine, she attempts to shoot him, but she only grazes his arm. The police show up, and Lieutenant Escobar fires a warning shot at Evelyn when she endeavors to make a getaway with Katherine by her side in her Packard. Another cop, who is clearly on Noah Cross's payroll, knocks Escobar out of the way and shoots to kill. There is a long shot of Evelyn's car at the opposite end of the street; her car stops and we hear her horn honking as her body falls forward and her head hits the steering wheel in death.

Everyone rushes to Evelyn's Packard while Cross shields Katherine from the sight of her mother's corpse. Cross announces that he intends to gain custody of the only daughter he has left. Gittes is overwhelmed by the death of Evelyn and the realization that Noah has gotten away with murder, fraud, and incest. His assistant, Walsh (Joe Mantell), advises, "Forget it, Jake; it's Chinatown." This is one of the most haunting closing lines of any film in motion picture history. Having endeavored to save Evelyn from her father, "he winds up getting her killed instead."[11] Earlier in the scene, Gittes had muttered, "You never know what's going on." Chinatown is inscrutable.

"Gittes is a very simple man," Kael writes. "Towne's heroes are like the heroes of hard-boiled fiction. They don't ask much of life."[12] And they sometimes don't even get that.

"What exerts a strangle hold on the viewer's mind for days afterward is the film's dark sense of misfortune." That is Polanski's hallmark.[13] Directors like Polanski brought with them to the United States a "doom-laden worldview," says Mark Osteen in *Nightmare Alley*. Polanski acquired his dark view of life while growing up in occupied Poland, and it is there in *Chinatown*.[14]

When it comes to a film that captures the atmosphere of Los Angeles, *Chinatown* is among the best. *Gangster Squad* (2013) is likewise a movie set in Los Angeles, and it aims to capture the flavor of the city. This sort of period gangster tale is "more elegantly told in such films as *Chinatown*,"[15] but *Gangster Squad* is still a worthwhile picture.

Gangster Squad (2013)

Gangster Squad originated in 2008, in a series of articles in the *Los Angeles Times* by Paul Lieberman about the real gangster squad, which was created after World War II by police chief William Parker. He was determined to root out gangsters the likes of Meyer "Mickey" Cohen, often by such morally ambiguous means as illegal wire taps and roughing up suspects during interrogations. "Tommy gun-wielding cops" appear in some scenes of the film, scenes that were so violent that the release of the movie was delayed from September 2012 to January 2013, so that some of the violence could be toned down. (As a matter of fact, the gangster squad seldom used their tommy guns in real life.[16]) Josh Brolin plays John O'Mara, the actual leader of the gangster squad, who was fundamentally honorable, but increasingly ruthless.

One of the scenes that was overhauled is set in Chinatown in the revised film, where the gangster squad has a shootout with Cohen's gang. "In some ways it's better," director Ruben Fleischer says of the revised version of the movie. "After all, some of the scenes are kind of tommy-gun heavy."[17]

Paul Lieberman states that *Gangster Squad* is set in 1949, the year that Warner Bros. released *White Heat*, the kind of gangster picture that "inspired" Mickey Cohen to be a big-time mobster. But Cohen was not an archetypal gangster like Cody Jarrott in *White Heat*, "who dies in a blaze of glory atop an oil refinery" (see chapter 5).[18]

The picture begins with a prologue narrated by Sergeant John O'Mara, voice-over on the sound track: "Mickey Cohen honed his skills as a boxer to climb the social ladder of the mob—a Jew who gained the respect of the mob by way of a homicidal lust for power. He wanted to own the town." The movie proper begins in 1949, with police chief William Parker (Nick Nolte) ordering Sergeant O'Mara to "wage guerilla warfare" against Mickey Cohen, who aims to rule the city of Los Angeles and replace Chicago as the center of gang activity in the United States. Chief Parker concludes, "We are losing L.A. to Cohen. Drive that bastard out of the city."

When O'Mara begins picking the members of his elite squad, his wife advises him that he is inclined to choose men who are too straight-laced, who go by the book: "You shouldn't be looking for choir boys, but tough guys." O'Mara's final choices include Sergeant Jerry Wooters (Ryan Gosling), whom O'Mara says is like an "Indian guide who knows the territory"—that is, the local crime scene (Jerry is also carrying on a clandestine affair with Grace Faraday [Emma Stone], Cohen's girlfriend); Officer Max Kennard (Robert Patrick), a gruff, Spartan gunslinger; and Officer Conwell Keeler (Giovanni Ribisi), who is the moral compass of the group. When O'Mara commands him to install a bug in Cohen's mansion without a judge's warrant to make it legal, Keeler says to O'Mara, "I'm having trouble seeing the difference between them and us." O'Mara responds, "This is the only way we can beat them!"

In Gangster Squad: *Tough Guys with Style*, the documentary featured on the *Gangster Squad* DVD, Josh Brolin explains, "What these guys had was conviction." To take down the bad guys they would sometimes act like bad guys. "There was a primitive set of standards that they lived by." They operated ruthlessly and efficiently.[19] Director Ruben Fleischer says in the same documentary that the gangster squad sometimes had to bend the rules, or break them now and then. This sounds like the rules that J. Edgar Hoover ordered Melvin Purvis to follow in *Public Enemies*, rules that Purvis thought to be dishonorable (see chapter 12). The question raised by Keeler and not adequately answered in the film is: If you stoop to the level of your enemy by adopting his underhanded tactics, do you become like him? Keeler seems to think so; O'Mara does not seem to be troubled by the question.

The gangster squad's campaign of attacking Cohen's rackets culminates in a raid on Cohen's bookmaking operation, a lucrative off-track betting setup. In retaliation, "Cohen lures the gangster squad to a booby-trapped truck in Chinatown, but they are unharmed."[20] However, Cohen's mob tracks down Conwell Keeler's hideaway and murders him. Cohen personally kills Wooter's pal, Jack Whalan (Sullivan Stapleton), for providing sanctuary for Grace Faraday. Nonetheless, Grace escapes and is reunited with Jerry. She promises that she will testify in court that she witnessed Cohen murder Whalan. O'Mara and his squad set out to arrest Cohen on the murder charge at the Park Plaza Hotel, which Cohen has turned into a fortress. It is the Christmas holiday as the gangster squad exchanges gunfire with Cohen's mob, and the Christmas decorations in the hotel lobby are shattered. Although one does not ordinarily associate guns with the Christmas season, Ruben Fleischer employs the Yuletide atmosphere as a jarring counterpoint to the violent events in the story.

After the gangster squad vanquishes Cohen's mob in the gunfight at the hotel, Cohen and O'Mara engage in a boxing match on the hotel grounds. But Cohen's boxing days are over, and O'Mara knocks him out cold. Chief Parker disbands the gangster squad and gets all the credit for ending the reign of Mickey Cohen in Los Angeles. O'Mara receives no mention for his role in the downfall of Cohen. By the time Mickey Cohen expired in 1976, he was a relic of Los Angeles's past, a hoodlum who failed to hold on to the notoriety he achieved in the underworld during the postwar years. At film's end, John O'Mara bids a fond farewell to his police career by tossing his badge into the Pacific Ocean.

Gangster Squad received mixed reviews but performed fairly well at the box office. Academy Award–winner Sean Penn (*Mystic River*, *Milk*) was acclaimed for inhabiting the role of Mickey Cohen rather than giving a cliché-ridden performance as a gangster. "The film is mostly well cast, and Ryan Gosling is particularly effective as the cynical pretty boy."[21]

* * *

As I declared at the beginning of this afterword, "Time marches on," so I present a postscript on the increased accessibility of earlier gangster films on DVD, whereas in the past only marquee titles and established classics were likely to be available. These lesser-known but worthwhile movies can now be obtained on a "manufactured on-demand disc." According to Michael Cardullo, of the Warner Archive Collection, this is a way of "shining a light on things people otherwise wouldn't have access to"—for example, Joseph Lewis's masterful *Gun Crazy* (1950). There are also precode gangster films, made before the Motion Picture Production Code of 1930 was finally enforced in 1934; *Beast of the City* (1931), with Jean Harlow, is one example. The Warner Archive Collection includes films from RKO and MGM, so film fans can see older, even forgotten, films of the past, as well as keep abreast of recent gangster films.[22]

Josef von Sternberg's *Underworld* (1927) helped to establish the mob boss, "devilishly tommy-gunning his way through the wet, studio-set streets."[23] Then came the cycle of gangster pictures in the 1930s, and the resurrection of the genre after World War II. And so the gangster genre continues to march on. A stock question raised by gangster pictures is: why do people become criminals? According to Thomas Leitch, the reasons include "alienation from a remote and uncaring society, combined with an overreaching vanity or megalomania." Criminal behavior, he continues, is rooted in "ethnic self-identification, and vaulting personal ambition" (starting with *Little Caesar* and *Public Enemies*), and the "fatal need for the company of others" (*The Asphalt Jungle*), when the gang is assembled like a pick-up ball team to pull off a big job.[24]

The mass audience continues to be fascinated by individuals who choose to be criminals, from Bull Weed in *Underworld* to Mickey Cohen in *Gangster Squad*. Whether in films set in contemporary America, like *The Grifters*, or films that harken back to earlier periods, for example, *Bonnie and Clyde* and *Chinatown*, the gangster genre will continue to flourish in the future as it has in the past.

NOTES

Introduction

1. Marilyn Yaquinto, *Pump 'Em Full of Lead: A Look at Gangsters on Film* (New York: Twayne, 1998), xi.

2. Jack Shadoian, *Dreams and Dead Ends: The American Gangster Film*, 2nd ed. (New York: Oxford University Press, 2003), 3.

3. Colin McArthur, *Underworld USA* (New York: Viking, 1972), 8.

Chapter One

1. Ralph Bauer, "When the Lights Went Out: Hollywood, the Depression, and the Thirties," in *Movies as Artifacts: Cultural Criticism of Popular Film*, Michael T. Marsden, John Nachbar, and Sam L. Grogg, eds. (Chicago: Nelson-Hall, 1982), 39.

2. See Thomas Leitch, *Crime Films* (2002; reprint, New York: Cambridge University Press, 2009), 20–23.

3. Robert Warshow, "The Gangster as Tragic Hero," in *The Immediate Experience: Movies, Comics, Theater, and Other Aspects of Popular Culture* (Cambridge, Mass.: Harvard University Press, 2001), 102.

4. Marilyn Yaquinto, *Pump 'Em Full of Lead: A Look at Gangsters on Film* (New York: Twayne, 1998), 11.

5. Jonathan Munby, *Public Enemies, Public Heroes: Screening the Gangster from Little Caesar to Touch of Evil* (Chicago: University of Chicago Press, 1999), 24.

6. Yaquinto, *Pump 'Em Full of Lead*.

7. John Tibbetts, "Josef von Sternberg," in *Encyclopedia of Filmmakers*, vol. 2, James Welsh and John Tibbetts, eds. (New York: Facts on File, 2002), 655.

8. James Poniewozik, "The Original Jersey Shore," *Time*, September 27, 2010, 63.

9. Ben Hecht, "The Front Page: Now and Then," November 18, 1961, Ben Hecht Papers, Newberry Library, Chicago.

10. Dave Kehr, "Von Sternberg: Chief Director of Private Dream Factory," *New York Times*, August 20, 2010, sec. 2, 10.

11. Fran Mason, *American Gangster Cinema: From* Little Caesar *to* Pulp Fiction (New York: Palgrave Macmillan, 2002), 4.

12. Mason, *American Gangster Cinema*, 4.

13. Bryan Foy, interview with the author, Los Angeles, California, September 4, 1975.

Chapter Two

1. MarilynYaquinto, *Pump 'Em Full of Lead: A Look at Gangsters on Film* (New York: Twayne, 1998), 29.

2. Ken Mate and Patrick McGilligan, "W. R. Burnett: The Outsider," in *Backstory: Interviews with Screenwriters of Hollywood's Golden Age*, vol. 1, Patrick McGilligan, ed. (Los Angeles: University of California Press, 1986), 56.

3. Greg S. Faller, "*Little Caesar*," in *International Dictionary of Films and Filmmakers*, rev. ed., vol. 1, Nicolet Elert, Andrew Sarris, and Grace Jeromski, eds. (New York: St. James Press, 2000), 581.

4. Jack Shadoian, *Dreams and Dead Ends: The American Gangster Film* (New York: Oxford University Press, 2003), 47.

5. Gregory Black, *Hollywood Censored: Morality Codes, Catholics, and the Movies* (New York: Cambridge University Press, 1994).

6. Black, *Hollywood Censored*, 118.

7. Vito Russo, *The Celluloid Closet: Homosexuality in the Movies* (New York: Harper & Row, 1987), 46.

8. Les Keyser and Barbara Keyser, *Hollywood and the Catholic Church: The Image of Roman Catholicism in American Movies* (Chicago: Loyola University Press, 1984), 45.

9. Kathryn Osenlund, "*Little Caesar*," in *Encyclopedia of Novels into Film*, vol. 1, James M. Welsh and John Tibbetts, eds. (New York: Facts on File, 2005), 250.

10. Steve Hanson, "*The Public Enemy*," in *International Dictionary of Films and Filmmakers*, vol. 1, Nicolet Elert, Andrew Sarris, and Grace Jeromski, eds. (New York: St. James Press, 2000), 877.

11. Curtis Lee Hanson, "William Wellman: A Memorable Visit with an Elder Statesman," *Cinema* 3 (July 1966): 22.

12. Martin Scorsese in Karen Hillhouse and John Rust, *Beer and Blood: Enemies of the Public* (Valencia, Calif.: Taylormade Entertainment, 2000), DVD.

13. John Tibbetts, "William Wellman," in *Encyclopedia of Filmmakers*, vol. 2, James M. Welsh and John Tibbetts, eds. (New York: Facts on File, 2002), 675.

14. Black, *Hollywood Censored*, 116.

15. Harvey Thew, *The Public Enemy: A Screenplay*, Henry Cohen, ed. (Madison: University of Wisconsin Press, 1981), 99.

16. *Production Code of the Motion Picture Association of America*, "To Govern the Making of Motion Pictures," 9–10. Production Code Administration Archives at the Margaret Herrick Library of the Motion Picture Academy, Beverly Hills, California.

17. Carlos Clarens, *Crime Movies: An Illustrated History of the Genre from D. W. Griffith to* Pulp Fiction, rev. ed. (New York: Da Capo, 1997), 60.

18. Lincoln Kirstein, "James Cagney and the American Hero," *Hound and Horn* (April/June 1932), in *American Film Criticism*, Stanley Kaufman and Bruce Henstell, eds. (New York: Liveright, 1972), 263–64.

19. James Hamilton, *"The Public Enemy," National Board of Review Magazine* (May 1931), in *American Film Criticism*, Stanley Kaufman and Bruce Henstell, eds. (New York: Liveright, 1972), 252.

20. Drew Casper in Karen Hillhouse and John Rust, *Beer and Blood: Enemies of the Public* (Valencia, Calif.: Taylormade Entertainment, 2000), DVD.

21. Kirstein, "James Cagney and the American Hero," 264.

22. Hamilton, *"The Public Enemy,"* 252.

23. *"The Public Enemy," Variety*, April 29, 1931, 12.

Chapter Three

1. Carlos Clarens, *Crime Movies: An Illustrated History of the Genre from D. W. Griffith to* Pulp Fiction, rev. ed. (New York: Da Capo, 1997), 110–12.

2. William Faulkner, "Introduction," *Sanctuary* (New York: Vintage Books, 1991), 321.

3. David Vanderwekken, *"Sanctuary,"* in *A William Faulkner Encyclopedia,"* Robert W. Hamblin and Charles A. Peek, eds. (Westport, Conn.: Greenwood Press, 1999), 341.

4. Gregory Black, *Hollywood Censored: Morality Codes, Catholics, and the Movies* (New York: Cambridge University Press, 1994).

5. Gregory Black, *"Sanctuary,"* in *Encyclopedia of Novels into Film*, vol. 1, James M. Welsh and John Tibbetts, eds. (New York: Facts on File, 2005), 392.

6. Clarens, *Crime Movies*, 112.

7. Ephraim Katz, ed., with Peter Nolen, *Film Encyclopedia*, rev. ed. (New York: HarperCollins, 2008), 1,215.

8. Joseph Breen to Hays Office, March 17, 1933, Production Code Administration Archive.

9. Julian Petley, "Karl Struss," in *International Dictionary of Films and Filmmakers*, rev. ed., vol. 4, Nicolet Elert, Andrew Sarris, and Grace Jeromski, eds. (New York: St. James Press, 2000), 801.

10. Charles Higham and Joel Greenberg, "Jean Negulesco," in *The Celluloid Muse: Hollywood Directors Speak* (New York: New American Library, 1972), 210.

11. Clarens, *Crime Movies*, 112.

12. "*The Story of Temple Drake*," *Harrison Reports*, May 13, 1933, 3.

13. "*The Story of Temple Drake*," *Time*, May 15, 1933, 36.

14. Leslie Halliwell, "*The Story of Temple Drake*," in *Film Guide*, rev ed., David Critten, ed. (New York: HarperCollins, 2008), 1,136.

15. William K. Everson, unpublished program notes for *The Story of Temple Drake*, New School of Social Research, New York, March 24, 1971.

16. Dan Callahan, "Miriam Hopkins," *Sight and Sound* 22, no. 12 (December 2012): 36.

17. Richard Griffith and Arthur Mayer, *The Movies*, rev. ed. (New York: Simon & Schuster, 1970), 693.

18. Nick Pinkerton, "*Crime Doesn't Pay: The Complete Shorts Collection*," *Sight and Sound* 22, no. 11 (November 2012): 112.

19. George Orwell, "Raffles and Miss Blandish," in *Decline of the English Murder and Other Essays* (Harmondsworth, U.K.: Penguin, 1965), 68–69.

20. Quoted in Douglas Martin, "Joseph Blotner, Faulkner Expert, Dies," *New York Times*, November 23, 2012, sec. B, 7.

21. J. C. Robertson, *The Hidden Cinema: British Film Censorship in Action* (London: Routledge, 1989), 94.

22. P. Nobel, ed., *British Film Yearbook, 1949–50* (London: Skelton Robinson, 1949), 505.

23. Dave Kehr, "Thrills from British Vaults: *No Orchids for Miss Blandish*," *New York Times*, June 18, 2010, sec. 2, 13.

24. "*No Orchids for Miss Blandish*," *Picturegoer* (London), July 3, 1948, 13.

25. "*No Orchids for Miss Blandish*," *Monthly Film Bulletin* (April 1948): 47.

26. Brian McFarlane, "Outrage: *No Orchids for Miss Blandish*," in *British Crime Cinema*, Steve Chibnall and Robert Murphy, eds. (New York: Routledge, 1999), 39.

27. *Production Code of the Motion Picture Association of America*, 11. Production Code Administration Archives at the Margaret Herrick Library of the Motion Picture Academy, Beverly Hills, California.

28. St. John Clowes, *No Orchids for Miss Blandish*, Joel Greenberg TV interview with Richard Gordon (Tulsa, Okla.: VCI Entertainment, 2010), DVD.

29. Kehr, "Thrills from British Vaults," sec. 2, 13.

30. McFarlane, "Outrage," 46.

31. Leslie Halliwell, "*No Orchids for Miss Blandish*," in *Film Guide*, rev ed., David Critten, ed. (New York: HarperCollins, 2008), 853.

32. Brian McFarlane, "Linden Travers Interview," in *An Autobiography of British Cinema by the Actors and Filmmakers Who Made It* (London: Methuen/British Film Institute, 1997), 569.

Chapter Four

1. Robert Warshow, "The Gangster as Tragic Hero," in *The Immediate Experience: Movies, Comics, Theater, and Other Aspects of Popular Culture* (Cambridge, Mass.: Harvard University Press, 2001), 102.

2. Thomas Leitch, *Crime Films* (2002; reprint, New York: Cambridge University Press, 2009), 107.

3. Jan Herman, *A Talent for Trouble: The Life of Hollywood's Most Acclaimed Director, William Wyler* (New York: G. P. Putnam's Sons, 1995), 109.

4. Gregory Black, *Hollywood Censored: Morality Codes, Catholics, and the Movies* (New York: Cambridge University Press, 1994), 240.

5. Pauline Kael, "*Dead End*," *New Yorker*, September 11, 1995, 28.

6. Quoted in Scott Berg, *Goldwyn: A Biography* (New York: Knopf, 1989), 290.

7. Mike Cormack, *Ideology and Cinematography in Hollywood, 1930–39* (New York: St. Martin's Press, 1994), 126.

8. William Wyler, interview by the author, August 15, 1975.

9. Charles Afron, "William Wyler," in *International Dictionary of Films and Filmmakers*, rev. ed., vol. 2, Nicolet Elert, Andrew Sarris, and Grace Jeromski, eds. (New York: St. James Press, 2000), 567.

10. Edith Lee, "Richard Day," in *International Dictionary of Films and Filmmakers*, rev. ed., vol. 4, Nicolet Elert, Andrew Sarris, and Grace Jeromski, eds. (New York: St. James Press, 2000), 84–85.

11. Michael Aneregg, *William Wyler* (Boston: Twayne, 1979), 63.

12. Black, *Hollywood Censored*, 278, 280.

13. Carl Rollyson, *Lillian Hellman: Her Legend and Her Legacy* (New York: St. Martin's Press, 1988), 106.

14. Graham Greene, *The Graham Greene Film Reader: Reviews, Essays, Interviews, and Film Stories*, David Parkinson, ed. (New York: Applause Books, 1994), 240–41.

15. James Neibaur, *Tough Guys: The American Movie Macho* (Jefferson, N.C.: McFarland, 1989), 76.

16. Cormack, *Ideology and Cinematography in Hollywood*, 133.

17. Greene, *The Graham Greene Film Reader*, 427.

18. Black, *Hollywood Censored*, 280.

19. Anderegg, *William Wyler*, 64.

20. Gerald Mast and Bruce Kawin, *A Short History of the Movies*, rev. ed. (New York: Longman, 2008), 349.

21. Graham Greene, *A Gun for Sale* (New York: Penguin, 2005), ii.

22. Samuel Hynes, "Introduction," *A Gun for Sale*, xiv.

23. Judith Adamson, *Graham Greene and the Cinema* (Norman, Okla.: Pilgrim Books, 1984), 29.

24. David Thomson, *New Biographical Dictionary of Film*, rev. ed. (New York: Knopf, 2010), 910.

25. Brian Baxter, *"This Gun for Hire,"* in *Graham Greene and the Cinema*, program notes, National Film Theater, London, 1972, 23.

26. Graham Greene, interview by the author, Antibes, France, July 23, 1977.

27. Dave Kehr, "Dark Crimes," *New York Times*, December 9, 2012, sec. 2, 19.

28. Jack Edmund Nolan, "Graham Greene's Films," *Literature/Film Quarterly* 2, no. 4 (Fall 1974): 305.

29. Carlos Clarens, *Crime Movies: An Illustrated History of the Genre from D. W. Griffith to* Pulp Fiction, rev. ed. (New York: Da Capo, 1997), 180.

30. Philips Hartung, *"This Gun for Hire,"* *Commonweal*, May 29, 1942, 36–37.

Chapter Five

1. Thomas Leitch, *Crime Films* (2002; reprint, New York: Cambridge University Press, 2009), 33.

2. Gerald Mast and Bruce Kawin, *A Short History of the Movies*, rev. ed. (New York: Longman, 2008), 351.

3. Dave Kehr, "Dark Crimes," *New York Times*, December 9, 2012, sec. 2, 23.

4. Molly Haskell, "Film Forum," *New York Times Book Review*, December 16, 2012, 13.

5. Richard Ness, "Miklos Rozsa," in *International Dictionary of Films and Filmmakers*, rev. ed., vol. 4, Nicolet Elert, Andrew Sarris, and Grace Jeromski, eds. (New York: St. James Press, 2000), 724.

6. Robert Siodmak, "Hoodlums: The Myth," in *Hollywood Directors: 1941–71*, Richard Koszarski, ed. (New York: Oxford University Press, 1971), 286.

7. Colin McArthur, *Underworld USA* (New York: Viking, 1972), 109.

8. Jack Shadoian, *Dreams and Dead Ends: The American Gangster Film* (New York: Oxford University Press, 2003), 308, 310.

9. Shadoian, *Dreams and Dead Ends*, 320.

10. Jay Cocks, "Ten Great Movies to Be Watched Over and Over," *TV Guide*, August 5, 1989, 11.

11. Karen Burroughs Hannsberry, *Bad Boys: The Actors of Film Noir* (Jefferson, N.C.: McFarland, 2003), 375.

12. Michael Barson, *The Illustrated Who's Who of Hollywood Directors* (New York: Noonday Press, 1995), 388.

13. Carlos Clarens, *Crime Movies: An Illustrated History of the Genre from D. W. Griffith to* Pulp Fiction, rev. ed. (New York: Da Capo, 1997), 180.

14. Leitch, *Crime Films*.

15. Pauline Kael, *Kiss Kiss Bang Bang* (New York: Bantam, 1969), 439.

16. Kael, *Kiss Kiss Bang Bang*, 319.

17. Michael Atkinson, "Recent Releases: *Pursued*," *Sight and Sound* 22, no. 8 (August 2012): 117.

18. Mast and Kawin, *A Short History of the Movies*, 351.

19. Martin Scorsese, *White Heat: Top of the World* (Valencia, Calif.: Taylor-made Entertainment, 2005), DVD.

20. Jonathan Munby, *Public Enemies, Public Heroes: Screening the Gangster from* Little Caesar *to* Touch of Evil (Chicago: University of Chicago Press, 1999), 115–16.

21. Marilyn Yaquinto, *Pump 'Em Full of Lead: A Look at Gangsters on Film* (New York: Twayne, 1998), 81.

22. Joseph Milicia, "Max Steiner," in *International Dictionary of Films and Filmmakers*, rev. ed., vol. 4, Nicolet Elert, Andrew Sarris, and Grace Jeromski, eds. (New York: St. James Press, 2000), 790.

23. Scorsese, *White Heat*.

24. Drew Casper, audio commentary, Martin Scorsese, *White Heat: Top of the World* (Valencia, Calif.: Taylormade Entertainment, 2005), DVD.

25. John McCarty, *Hollywood Gangland: The Movies' Love Affair with the Mob* (New York: St. Martin's Press, 1993), 98.

26. Leitch, *Crime Films*, 227–28.

27. Ed Lowry, "*White Heat*," in *International Dictionary of Films and Filmmakers*, rev. ed., vol. 1, Nicolet Elert, Andrew Sarris, and Grace Jeromski, eds. (New York: St. James Press, 2000), 1,091.

28. Lowry, "*White Heat*," 1,091.

Chapter Six

1. See Thomas Erskine, "*Key Largo*," in *Video Versions: Film Adaptations of Plays on Video*, James M. Welsh and Thomas Erskine, eds. (Westport, Conn.: Greenwood Press, 2000), 178.

2. John Huston, interview by the author, London, July 31, 1972. All quotations from Huston that are not attributed to another source are from this interview.

3. "Key Largo," in *Motion Picture Guide: 1927–83*, vol. 4, Jay Robert Nash and Stanley Ralph Ross, eds. (Chicago: Cinebooks, 1985), 1,514. The pages are numbered consecutively throughout the twelve volumes.

4. Thomas Leitch, *Crime Films* (2002; reprint, New York: Cambridge University Press, 2009), 31.

5. Scott Hammen, *John Huston* (Boston: Twayne, 1985), 42–43.

6. John McCarty, *The Films of John Huston* (Secaucus, N.J.: Citadel Press, 1987), 67.

7. John Tibbetts, "*Key Largo*," in *Encyclopedia of Stage Plays into Film*, James M. Welsh and John Tibbetts, eds. (New York: Facts on File, 2001), 168.

8. Carlos Clarens, *Crime Movies: An Illustrated History of the Genre from D. W. Griffith to Pulp Fiction*, rev. ed. (New York: Da Capo, 1997), 225.

9. "John Huston and *Key Largo*," *Time*, August 2, 1948, 74.

10. Thomas Doherty, *Hollywood's Censor: Joseph Breen* (New York: Columbia University Press, 2007), 267–68.

11. John Huston, *An Open Book* (New York: Knopf, 1980), 151.

12. Hammen, *John Huston*, 43.

13. Hammen, *John Huston*, 42.

14. Barry Gifford, *The Devil Thumbs a Ride and Other Unforgettable Films* (New York: Grove Press, 1988), 88.

15. "*Key Largo*," *Motion Picture Guide*, 1,514.

16. Huston, *An Open Book*, 150.

17. Jonathan Munby, *Public Enemies, Public Heroes: Screening the Gangster from Little Caesar to Touch of Evil* (Chicago: University of Chicago Press, 1999), 143.

18. John McCarty, *Hollywood Gangland: The Movies' Love Affair with the Mob* (New York: St. Martin's Press, 1993), 157.

19. Dennis Lim, "It's All about a Dishonest Day's Work," *New York Times*, October 1, 2010, sec. 2, 1.

20. Karel Reisz, "Interview with Huston," in *John Huston: Interviews*, Robert Emmet Long, ed. (Jackson: University Press of Mississippi, 2001), 4.

21. Quoted in Hammen, *John Huston*, 53.

22. Drew Casper, audio commentary track, John Huston, *The Asphalt Jungle* (Burbank, Calif.: Warner Bros., 2004), DVD.

23. Lawrence Grobel, *The Hustons* (New York: Scribner's, 1989), 335.

24. *Production Code of the Motion Picture Association of America*, "To Govern the Making of Motion Pictures," 2. Production Code Administration Archives at the Margaret Herrick Library of the Motion Picture Academy, Beverly Hills, California.

25. Huston, *An Open Book*, 84.

26. Hammen, *John Huston*, 50.

27. McCarty, *Hollywood Gangland*, 157.

28. Philip Kemp, "*The Asphalt Jungle*," in *International Dictionary of Films and Filmmakers*, rev. ed., vol. 1, Nicolet Elert, Andrew Sarris, and Grace Jeromski, eds. (New York: St. James Press, 2000), 70.

29. Munby, *Public Enemies, Public Heroes*, 137–38.

30. Quoted in Grobel, *The Hustons*, 336.

31. Quoted in Grobel, *The Hustons*, 336–37.

32. Quoted in Clarens, *Crime Movies*, 203.

Chapter Seven

1. Leslie Megahey, "Interview from *The Orson Welles Story*," in *Orson Welles: Interviews*, Mark W. Estrin, ed. (Jackson: University Press of Mississippi, 2002), 192.

2. Thomas Erskine, "*The Lady from Shanghai*," in *Encyclopedia of Orson Welles*, Chuck Berg and Thomas Erskine, eds. (New York: Facts on File, 2002), 282.

3. Tom Conley, "*The Lady from Shanghai*," in *International Dictionary of Films and Filmmakers*, rev. ed., vol. 1, Nicolet Elert, Andrew Sarris, and Grace Jeromski, eds. (New York: St. James Press, 2000), 347.

4. Conley, "*The Lady from Shanghai*," 347.

5. Orson Welles and Peter Bogdanovich, *This Is Orson Welles*, rev. ed. (New York: Da Capo, 1998), 193.

6. Welles and Bogdanovich, *This Is Orson Welles*, 193.

7. J. P. Telotte, "Film Noir and Columbia," *Columbia Pictures: Portrait of a Studio*, Bernard F. Dick, ed. (Lexington: University Press of Kentucky, 1992), 110.

8. Charles Higham, *The Films of Orson Welles* (Los Angeles: University of California Press, 1973), 112. Higham published a revised edition of this book in 1985, but the original edition is still revered as a milestone in Welles scholarship by demonstrating that Welles was a major cinematic artist.

9. Clinton Heylin, *Despite the System: Orson Welles versus the Hollywood Studios* (Chicago: Review Press, 2005), 213, 221. Heylin has the occasional howler, as when he says that Erskine Sanford played Arthur Bannister in the film, instead of Everett Sloane, 222.

10. Welles and Bogdanovich, *This Is Orson Welles*, 402–3.

11. Erskine, "*The Lady from Shanghai*," 207.

12. Andrew Britton, "Betrayed by Rita: *The Lady from Shanghai*," in *The Book of Film Noir*, Ian Cameron, ed. (New York: Continuum, 1992), 221.

13. *Production Code of the Motion Picture Association of America*, 3. Production Code Administration Archives at the Margaret Herrick Library of the Motion Picture Academy, Beverly Hills, California.

14. Heylin, *Despite the System*, 217.

15. J. P. Telotte, *Voices in the Dark: The Narrative Patterns of Film Noir* (Champaign: University of Illinois Press, 1989), 66.

16. Raymond Borde and Etienne Chaumeton, *A Panorama of American Film Noir, 1941–53*, Paul Hammon, trans. (San Francisco: City Lights Books, 2002), 63. This is the first major study of film noir in French.

17. Kelly Oliver, *Noir Anxiety* (Minneapolis: University of Minnesota Press, 2003), 67–69. Cantonese translations by Jiahui Li.

18. Conley, "*The Lady from Shanghai*," 548.

19. Peter Bogdanovich, commentary, Orson Welles, *The Lady from Shanghai* (Culver City, Calif.: Columbia Tri-Star Home Video, 2000), DVD.

20. Richard Corliss, "The Man Did Make Movies," *Time*, October 21, 1985, 100.

21. David Thomson, *Rosebud: The Story of Orson Welles* (New York: Vintage Books, 1997), 279.

22. Matthew Bruccoli, "Gerlach and Gatsby," *A Fitzgerald/Hemingway Annual* 7 (1975): 33–34.

23. DeWitt Bodeen, "F. Scott Fitzgerald and Film," *Films in Review* 28 (1977): 287; see also Philip Kemp, "The Five Key Fitzgerald Films," *Sight and Sound* 23, no. 6 (June 2013): 13.

24. Quoted in Guilia D'Agnola Vallon, "Last Neo-Traditionalist Standing," *Film Comment* 49, no. 1 (January–February 2013): 58.

25. Irene Atkins, "In Search of the Greatest Gatsby," *Literature/Film Quarterly* 3, no. 3 (Summer 1974): 218.

26. Elliott Nugent, *Events Leading Up to the Comedy: An Autobiography* (New York: Trident Press, 1965), 213–14.

27. Quoted in Atkins, "In Search of the Greatest Gatsby," 217.

28. Quoted in Ralph Wolfe, "Ladd," *Journal of Popular Film* 7, no. 4 (1980): 459.

29. Atkins, "In Search of the Greatest Gatsby," 220.

30. See James Miller, *F. Scott Fitzgerald: His Art and His Technique* (New York: New York University Press, 1967), 123.

31. Sara Mayfield, *Exiles from Paradise: F. Scott and Zelda Fitzgerald* (New York: Dell, 1974), 86.

32. Maxwell Perkins, "Maxwell Perkins to F. Scott Fitzgerald, November 24, 1924," in *Dear Scott/Dear Max: The Fitzgerald–Perkins Correspondence*, John Kuehl and Jackson Byer, eds. (New York: Scribner's, 1971), 82–83.

33. F. Scott Fitzgerald, *The Great Gatsby* (1925; reprint, New York: Scribner's, 2004), 159–60.

34. Manny Farber, "East Egg on the Face," in *Farber on Film: Film Writings of Manny Farber*, Robert Polito, ed. (New York: Library of America, 2009), 349.

35. Atkins, "In Search of the Greatest Gatsby," 226.

36. Charles McGrath, "Fitzgerald as Screenwriter: No Hollywood Ending," *New York Times*, April 22, 2004, sec. A, 1, 23; see also Rodney Richey, "The Other Authors of *Gone with the Wind*," in *American Classic Screen: Features*, James M. Welsh and John Tibbretts, eds. (Lanham, Md.: Scarecrow Press, 2010), 184–85. Fitzgerald was one of several writers who polished the shooting script of *Gone with the Wind*.

37. Nugent, *Events Leading Up to the Comedy*, 215.

38. Charles McGrath, "An Orgiastic *Gatsby*? Of Course," *New York Times*, May 3, 2013, sec. 2, 2.

Chapter Eight

1. Pauline Kael, *Kiss Kiss Bang Bang* (New York: Bantam, 1969), 61.

2. Lotte Eisner, *Fritz Lang*, Gertrud Monder, trans. (New York: Oxford University Press, 1977), 177.

3. Matthew Bernstein, *Walter Wanger, Hollywood Independent* (Berkeley: University of California Press, 1994), 119.

4. Quoted in Jeff Laffel, "Sylvia Sidney," *Films in Review* 45, nos. 9/10 (September–October 1994): 12.

5. Hilda Rolfe, "The Perfectionist," *Film Comment* 28, no. 6 (November–December 1992): 3.

6. Patrick McGilligan, *Fritz Lang: The Nature of the Beast* (New York: St. Martin's Press, 1997), 245.

7. Tom Gunning, *The Films of Fritz Lang: Allegories of Vision and Modernity* (London: British Film Institute, 2000), 238.

8. Kate Stables, "*You Only Live Once*," *Sight and Sound* 22, no. 7 (July 2012): 121.

9. Quoted in Michel Ciment et al., "Fritz Lang in Venice," in *Fritz Lang: Interviews*, Barry Grant, ed. (Jackson: University Press of Mississippi, 2003), 93.

10. Eisner, *Fritz Lang*, 185.

11. Quoted in Peter Bogdanovich, *Who the Devil Made It: Conversations with Film Directors* (New York: Knopf, 1997), 183.

12. James Parrish and Michael Pitts, *The Great Gangster Pictures* (Metuchen, N.J.: Scarecrow, 1976), 423.

13. Stables, *"You Only Live Once,"* 121.

14. Quoted in Bogdanovich, *Who the Devil Made It*, 35.

15. Quoted in Laffel, "Sylvia Sidney," 13.

16. Fritz Lang, interview by the author, Beverly Hills, June 9, 1971. All quotes from Fritz Lang that are not attributed to another source are from this interview.

17. Pauline Kael, *"You Only Live Once,"* *New Yorker*, July 24, 1995, 25.

18. Thomas Doherty, *Hollywood's Censor: Joseph Breen* (New York: Columbia University Press, 2007), 116.

19. Marilyn Yaquinto, *Pump 'Em Full of Lead: A Look at Gangsters on Film* (New York: Twayne, 1998), 75.

20. Gerald Mast and Bruce Kawin, *A Short History of the Movies*, rev. ed. (New York: Longman, 2008), 319.

21. Charles Higham and Joel Greenberg, "Interview with Fritz Lang," in *Fritz Lang: Interviews*, Barry Grant, ed. (Jackson: University of Mississippi Press, 2003), ii.

22. Frederick Ott, *The Films of Fritz Lang* (Secaucus, N.J.: Citadel Press, 1979), 246.

23. Gerard Leblanc and Brigette Devismes, *Le Double Scenario chez Fritz Lang* (Paris: Armand Colin, 1999), 205. Passage translated by Tom Gunning.

24. Ott, *The Films of Fritz Lang*, 253.

25. Colin McArthur, *The Big Heat* (London: British Film Institute, 1992), 50.

26. Kim Newman, *"The Big Heat,"* in *International Dictionary of Films and Filmmakers*, rev. ed., vol. 1, Nicolet Elert, Andrew Sarris, and Grace Jeromski, eds. (New York: St. James Press, 2000), 114.

27. McGilligan, *Fritz Lang*, 406.

28. Andy Klein, "Fritz Lang," *American Film* 14, no. 12 (October 1990): 58.

29. McArthur, *The Big Heat*, 69, 74.

30. William McGivern, "Flashback: Roman Holiday," *American Film* 8, no. 12 (October 1983): 47.

31. Gunning, *The Films of Fritz Lang*, 425.

32. McArthur, *The Big Heat*, 77.

33. Nick Pinkerton, "Lang the Defiant," *Sight and Sound* 23, no. 1 (January 2013): 113.

Chapter Nine

1. Gerald Mast and Bruce Kawin, *A Short History of the Movies*, rev. ed. (New York: Longman, 2008), 579.

2. Carlos Clarens, *Crime Movies: An Illustrated History of the Genre from D. W. Griffith to* Pulp Fiction, rev. ed. (New York: Da Capo, 1997), 276.

3. Quoted in Michael Goodwin and Naomi Wise, *On the Edge: The Life and Times of Francis Coppola* (New York: Morrow, 1989), 162.

4. Commentary, Francis Ford Coppola, *Godfather Collection* (Los Angeles, Calif.: Paramount, 2001), DVD. The DVD set of the *Godfather* trilogy contains a documentary on the making of the films and an audio commentary track by Coppola for each film. I refer to these items because they contain information not available anywhere else.

5. Ronald Bergan, *Francis Ford Coppola* (New York: Orion, 1998), 48, 163.

6. Mario Puzo, *The Godfather* (1969; reprint, New York: Penguin, 2002), 194–228.

7. William Murray, "*Playboy* Interview: Francis Ford Coppola," in *Francis Ford Coppola: Interviews*, Gene Phillips and Rodney Hill, eds. (Jackson: University Press of Mississippi, 2004), 31.

8. Coppola, *Godfather Collection*.

9. Richard Coombs, "Coppola's Family Plot," *Film Comment* 38, no. 2 (March–April 2002): 44.

10. Pauline Kael, *For Keeps: 30 Years at the Movies* (New York: Penguin, 1996), 595–96.

11. Marilyn Yaquinto, *Pump 'Em Full of Lead: A Look at Gangsters on Film* (New York: Twayne, 1998), 135.

12. Michael Pye and Linda Myers, *The Movie Brats: How the Film Generation Took Over Hollywood* (New York: Holt, Rinehart, and Winston, 1979), 106.

13. Alessandro Camon, "The *Godfather* and the Mythology of Mafia," *Francis Ford Coppola's Godfather Trilogy*, Nick Browne, ed. (New York: Cambridge University Press, 2000), 169.

14. See Les Keyser and Barbara Keyser, *Hollywood and the Catholic Church: The Image of Roman Catholicism in American Movies* (Chicago: Loyola University Press, 1984), 88.

15. Francis Ford Coppola, interview by the author, Cannes International Film Festival, May 20, 1979. All quotes from Coppola not attributed to another source are from this interview.

16. Coppola, *Godfather Collection*.

17. Kael, *For Keeps*, 595.

18. Nick Browne, "Violence as History in the *Godfather* Films," in *Francis Ford Coppola's Godfather Trilogy*, Nick Browne, ed. (New York: Cambridge University Press, 2000), 114.

19. Quoted in Harlan Lebo, *The Godfather Legacy* (New York: Simon & Schuster, 1997), 216.

20. Yaquinto, *Pump 'Em Full of Lead*, 140.

21. See Jenny Jones, ed., *The Annotated Godfather* (New York: Black Dog and Leventhall, 2007), 208.

22. Robert Johnson, *Francis Ford Coppola* (Boston: Twayne, 1977), 155.

23. Robert Warshow, "The Gangster as Tragic Hero," in *The Immediate Experience: Movies, Comics, Theater, and Other Aspects of Popular Culture* (Cambridge, Mass.: Harvard University Press, 2001), 132.

24. Quoted in Peter Biskind, *The Godfather Companion* (New York: Harper-Collins, 1990), 114.

25. Rodney Hill, "*Godfather II*," in *The Francis Ford Coppola Encyclopedia*, James M. Welsh, Gene Phillips, and Rodney Hill, eds. (Lanham, Md.: Scarecrow, 2010), 1–14.

26. Kael, *For Keeps*, 600.

27. A. O. Scott, "Seen This Guy Lately? Al Pacino," *New York Times*, April 2, 2003, sec. 2, 11.

Chapter Ten

1. Thomas Leitch, *Crime Films* (2002; reprint, New York: Cambridge University Press, 2009), 41.

2. Quoted in Jeff Laffel, "Sylvia Sidney," *Films in Review* 45, nos. 9/10 (September–October 1994): 12.

3. Melena Rizzik, "Awkward Bedfellows," *New York Times*, February 14, 2013, sec. 6, 1.

4. Leitch, *Crime Films*, 41–42.

5. Edward Murray, *The Film Classics* (New York: Unger, 1978), 247.

6. Quoted in Jim Hillier, "Arthur Penn," in *Focus on Bonnie and Clyde*, John Cawalti, ed. (Englewood Cliffs, N.J.: Prentice Hall, 1973), 14.

7. Eric Schaefer, "Burnett Guffey," in *International Dictionary of Films and Filmmakers*, rev. ed., vol. 4, Nicolet Elert, Andrew Sarris, and Grace Jeromski, eds. (New York: St. James Press, 2000), 331.

8. Pauline Kael, *Kiss Kiss Bang Bang* (New York: Bantam, 1969), 77.

9. George Faller, "Dede Allen," in *International Dictionary of Films and Filmmakers*, rev. ed., vol. 4, Nicolet Elert, Andrew Sarris, and Grace Jeromski, eds. (New York: St. James Press, 2000), 18.

10. Thomas Doherty, *Hollywood's Censor: Joseph Breen* (New York: Columbia University Press, 2007), 333.

11. Leland Poague, *"Bonnie and Clyde,"* in *International Dictionary of Films and Filmmakers*, rev. ed., vol. 1, Nicolet Elert, Andrew Sarris, and Grace Jeromski, eds. (New York: St. James Press, 2000), 143.

12. Peter Biskind, "Arthur Penn," *Sight and Sound* 20, no. 2 (December 2010): 36.

13. Anthony Schillaci, *"Bonnie and Clyde:* A Catholic Comment," *Film Comment* 4, no. 3 (Summer 1968): 49.

14. Jack Shadoian, *Dreams and Dead Ends: The American Gangster Film* (New York: Oxford University Press, 2003), 244.

15. John Kobler, *Capone* (New York: Da Capo, 1971), 23.

16. Michael Phillips, "Audiences Love a Bad Guy," *Chicago Tribune*, January 11, 2013, sec. 4, 6.

17. Roger Ebert, *"The Untouchables,"* in *Movie Home Companion* (New York: Andrews, McMeel and Parker, 2000), 630.

18. Phillips, "Audiences Love a Bad Guy," 6.

19. Ebert, *"The Untouchables,"* 630.

20. Gerald Mast and Bruce Kawin, *A Short History of the Movies*, rev. ed. (New York: Longman, 2008), 207.

21. Brian De Palma, commentary, Laurent Bouzereau, "Re-Inventing the Genre: *The Untouchables"* (Los Angeles, Calif.: Paramount, 2004), DVD. Unless otherwise noted, all quotes from the director come from this source.

22. John McCarty, *Hollywood Gangland: The Movies' Love Affair with the Mob* (New York: St. Martin's Press, 1993), 76.

23. See Ronald Koziol and Edward Baumann, "How Frank Nitti Met His Fate," *Chicago Tribune*, June 29, 1987, sec. 4, 1.

24. See Laura Shapiro and Ray Sawhill, "The First Untouchable," *Newsweek*, June 22, 1987, 68.

Chapter Eleven

1. Charles McGrath, "Filmed to a Pulp," *New York Times*, June 6, 2010, sec. 2, 1.

2. Douglas Brode, *Money, Women, and Guns: Crime Movies from* Bonnie and Clyde *to the Present* (New York: Carol, 1995), 178.

3. Joseph Bevan, "The Nothing Man: Jim Thompson," *Sight and Sound* 20, no. 6 (June 2010): 46.

4. Stephen Frears, commentary, *Making The Grifters*, part of Stephen Frears, *The Grifters* (Santa Monica, Calif.: Miramax, 2007), DVD. Includes interviews

with cast and crew members. Unless stated otherwise, all quotes from cast and crew come from this source.

5. Jane Haspel, "*The Grifters*," in *Encyclopedia of Novels into Film*, vol. 1, James M. Welsh and John Tibbetts, eds. (New York: Facts on File, 2005), 169.

6. Tom Orman, "*The Grifters*," in *International Dictionary of Films and Filmmakers*, rev. ed., vol. 1, Nicolet Elert, Andrew Sarris, and Grace Jeromski, eds. (New York: St. James Press, 2000), 416.

7. Haspel, "*The Grifters*," 169.

8. Thomas Leitch, *Crime Movies* (2002; reprint, New York: Cambridge University Press, 2009), 114.

9. Quoted in Brode, *Money, Women, and Guns*, 119.

10. Les Keyser, *Martin Scorsese* (Boston: Twayne, 1992), 12.

11. Keyser, *Martin Scorsese*, 14.

12. A. O. Scott, "Finding Drama in New-Fangled Filmmaking," *New York Times*, August 31, 2012, sec. C, 1.

13. Martin Scorsese, commentary, Gidion Phillips and Barbara Toennies, *Stranger Than Fiction: The True Story of Whitey Bulger, Southie, and* The Departed, part of Martin Scorsese, *The Departed*, two-disc special edition (Burbank, Calif.: Warner Bros., 2006), DVD. Unless stated otherwise, all quotes from Scorsese come from this source.

14. Michael Leyden, unpublished essay on *The Departed*, Loyola University of Chicago, 2010, 2–4.

15. Jess Bidgood, "James 'Whitey' Bulger Faces Racketeering Trial," *New York Times*, May 3, 2013, sec. 1, 13.

16. Martin Scorsese, interview with the author, New York City, July 28, 1975.

17. Leslie Halliwell, "*The Departed*," in *Film Guide*, rev. ed., David Critten, ed. (New York: HarperCollins, 2008), 309. Editor David Critten cites various reviews of the movie.

18. Leonard Maltin, ed., *Leonard Maltin's Classic Movie Guide*, 2nd ed. (New York: Plume, 2010), 343.

19. Gerald Mast and Bruce Kawin, *A Short History of the Movies*, rev. ed. (New York: Longman, 2008), 532.

Chapter Twelve

1. Philip Yordan, audio commentary, Max Nosseck, *Dillinger* (Burbank, Calif.: Warner Bros., 2005), DVD. Unless stated otherwise, all quotes from Yordan are from this source.

2. John McCarty, *Hollywood Gangland: The Movies' Love Affair with the Mob* (New York: St. Martin's Press, 1993), 129.

3. Quoted in Lee Server, "The Last Gangster: Marc Lawrence," *Film Comment* 33, no. 3 (May–June 1997): 67.

4. Marilyn Yaquinto, *Pump 'Em Full of Lead: A Look at Gangsters on Film* (New York: Twayne, 1998), 90.

5. John Milius, audio commentary, Max Nosseck, *Dillinger* (Burbank, Calif.: Warner Bros., 2005), DVD. Unless stated otherwise, all quotes from Milius are from this source.

6. Yaquinto, *Pump 'Em Full of Lead*, 89–90.

7. Jonathan Munby, *Public Enemies, Public Heroes: Screening the Gangster from* Little Caesar *to* Touch of Evil (Chicago: University of Chicago Press, 1999), 151–52.

8. *"Dillinger," Variety*, March 12, 1945, 8.

9. *"Dillinger," Hollywood Reporter*, March 12, 1945, 1.

10. John Ahearn, "Michael Mann," in *Encyclopedia of Filmmakers*, vol. 2, James M. Welsh and John Tibbetts, eds. (New York: Facts on File, 2002), 466.

11. Jed Dannenbaum, *Larger Than Life Adversaries*, part of Michael Mann, *Public Enemies*, two-disc special edition (Universal City, Calif.: Universal Pictures, 2009), DVD. This documentary includes interviews with cast and crew members. Unless noted otherwise, all quotes from cast and crew are from this source.

12. Michael Mann, audio commentary, Michael Mann, *Public Enemies*, two-disc special edition (Universal City, Calif.: Universal Pictures, 2009). Unless noted otherwise, all quotes from Mann are from this source.

13. McCarty, *Hollywood Gangland*, 129.

14. Bryan Burrough, "The Making of *J. Edgar*," *J. Edgar* (Burbank, Calif.: Warner Bros., 2011), DVD.

15. Christian Bale, commentary, Michael Mann, *Public Enemies*, two-disc special edition (Universal City, Calif.: Universal Pictures, 2009).

16. Carlos Clarens, *Crime Movies: An Illustrated History of the Genre from D. W. Griffith to* Pulp Fiction, rev. ed. (New York: Da Capo, 1997), 22–24.

17. Bale, *Public Enemies*.

18. Leonard Maltin, ed., *Leonard Maltin's Classic Movie Guide*, 2nd ed. (New York: Plume, 2010), 1,111.

19. Ahearn, "Michael Mann," 466.

Afterword

1. Quoted in Brooks Barnes and Bill Carter, "Newtown Massacre Changes Plans at Movie and TV Studios," *New York Times*, December 19, 2012, sec. C, 8.

2. Marilyn Yaquinto, *Pump 'Em Full of Lead: A Look at Gangsters on Film* (New York: Twayne, 1998), xii, 237.

3. Foster Hirsch, "Afterword," in *Crime Movies: An Illustrated History of the Genre from D. W. Griffith to* Pulp Fiction, rev. ed., Carlos Clarens, ed. (New York: Da Capo, 1997), 339.

4. Hirsch, "Afterword," 31.

5. Hirsch, "Afterword," 346.

6. Virginia Wright Wexman, *A History of Film*, 7th ed. (New York: Allyn & Bacon, 2010), 241.

7. Charles R. Berg, "Robert Towne," in *International Dictionary of Films and Filmmakers*, rev. ed., vol. 4, Nicolet Elert, Andrew Sarris, and Grace Jeromski, eds. (New York: St. James Press, 2000), 828–29.

8. Chinatown *Revisited with Roman Polanski, Robert Evans, and Robert Towne*, part of Roman Polanski, *Chinatown*, collector's edition (Los Angeles, Calif.: Paramount, 2006), DVD. Unless noted otherwise, all quotes from cast and crew are from this source.

9. Pauline Kael, *Reeling* (New York: Little, Brown, 1976), 969.

10. See Thomas Leitch, *Crime Films* (2002; reprint, New York: Cambridge University Press, 2009), 210.

11. John McCarty, "*Chinatown*," in *International Dictionary of Films and Filmmakers*, rev. ed., vol. 1, Nicolet Elert, Andrew Sarris, and Grace Jeromski, eds. (New York: St. James Press, 2000), 205.

12. Kael, *Reeling*, 585.

13. "Home Cinema," *Sight and Sound* 23, no. 5 (May 2013): 117.

14. Mark Osteen, *Nightmare Alley: Film Noir and the American Dream* (Baltimore, Md.: Johns Hopkins University Press, 2013), 111.

15. Duwane Dudek, "Penn Crackles in Violent *Gangster*," *Milwaukee Journal Sentinel*, January 11, 2013, sec. E, 3.

16. Michael Ciepley, "Rubbing Out the Mob in Los Angeles," *New York Times*, January 4, 2013, sec. 2, 1, 17.

17. Ruben Fleischer, commentary, Gangster Squad: *Tough Guys with Style*, part of Ruben Fleischer, *Gangster Squad* (Burbank, Calif.: Warner Bros., 2013), DVD.

18. Ciepley, "Rubbing Out the Mob in Los Angeles," 17.

19. Josh Brolin, commentary, Gangster Squad: *Tough Guys with Style*, part of Ruben Fleischer, *Gangster Squad* (Burbank, Calif.: Warner Bros., 2013), DVD.

20. Kate Stables, "*Gangster Squad*," *Sight and Sound* 23, no. 3 (March 2013): 96.

21. Dudek, "Penn Crackles in Violent *Gangster*," 3.

22. Dave Kehr, "A New Stream for the Thirsty," *New York Times*, May 26, 2013, sec. 2, 9, 13.

23. Michael Atkinson, "Moonshine Movies," *Sight and Sound* 22, no. 10 (October 2012): 36.

24. Leitch, *Crime Films*, 291–92.

BIBLIOGRAPHY

Adamson, Judith. *Graham Greene and Cinema*. Norman, Okla.: Pilgrim Books, 1984.

Anderegg, Michael. *William Wyler*. Boston: Twayne, 1979.

Armour, Robert A. *Fritz Lang*. Boston: Twayne, 1977.

Atkins, Irene. "In Search of the Greatest Gatsby." *Literature/Film Quarterly* 3, no. 3 (Summer 1974): 216–21.

Atkinson, Michael. "In the Magic Hour." *Sight and Sound* 22, no. 9 (September 2012): 84.

———. "Moonshine Movies." *Sight and Sound* 22, no. 10 (October 2012): 36–39.

———. "Recent Releases: *Pursued*." *Sight and Sound* 22, no. 8 (August 2012): 117.

Barnes, Brooks, and Bill Carter. "Newtown Massacre Changes Plans at Movie and TV Studios." *New York Times*, December 19, 2012, sec. C: 1, 8.

Barson, Michael. *The Illustrated Who's Who of Hollywood Directors*. New York: Noonday Press, 1995.

Berg, Chuck, and Thomas Erskine, eds. *Encyclopedia of Orson Welles*. New York: Facts on File, 2002.

Berg, Scott. *Goldwyn: A Biography*. New York: Knopf, 1989.

Bergan, Ronald. *Francis Ford Coppola*. New York: Orion, 1998.

Bernstein, Matthew. *Walter Wanger, Hollywood Independent*. Berkeley: University of California Press, 1994.

Bevan, Joseph. "The Nothing Man: Jim Thompson." *Sight and Sound* 20, no. 6 (June 2010): 46–49.

Bidgood, Jess. "James 'Whitey' Bulger Faces Racketeering Trial." *New York Times*, May 3, 2013, sec. 1: 13.

Biskind, Peter. "Arthur Penn." *Sight and Sound* 20, no. 2 (December 2010): 34–36.

———. *The Godfather Companion*. New York: HarperCollins, 1990.

Black, Gregory. *Hollywood Censored: Morality Codes, Catholics, and the Movies.* New York: Cambridge University Press, 1994.

Bodeen, DeWitt. "F. Scott Fitzgerald and Film." *Films in Review* 28 (1977): 287.

Bogdanovich, Peter. *Who the Devil Made It: Conversations with Film Directors.* New York: Knopf, 1997.

Borde, Raymond, and Etienne Chaumeton. *A Panorama of American Film Noir, 1941–53.* Paul Hammon, trans. San Francisco: City Lights Books, 2002.

Brode, Douglas. *Money, Women, and Guns: Crime Movies from* Bonnie and Clyde *to the Present.* New York: Carol, 1995.

Browne, Nick, ed. *Francis Ford Coppola's Godfather Trilogy.* New York: Cambridge University Press, 2000.

Bruccoli, Matthew. "Gerlach and Gatsby." *A Fitzgerald/Hemingway Annual* 7 (1975): 33–36.

Callahan, Dan. "Miriam Hopkins." *Sight and Sound* 22, no. 12 (December 2012): 36–39.

Cameron, Ian, ed. *The Book of Film Noir.* New York: Continuum, 1992.

Cawalti, John, ed. *Focus on Bonnie and Clyde.* Englewood Cliffs, N.J.: Prentice Hall, 1973.

Chibnall, Steve, and Robert Murphy, eds. *British Crime Cinema.* New York: Routledge, 1999.

Ciepley, Michael. "Rubbing Out the Mob in Los Angeles." *New York Times,* January 4, 2013, sec. 2: 1, 16, 17.

Clarens, Carlos. *Crime Movies: An Illustrated History of the Gangster Genre from D. W. Griffith to* Pulp Fiction, rev. ed. New York: Da Capo, 1997.

Coombs, Richard. "Coppola's Family Plot." *Film Comment* 38, no. 2 (March–April 2002): 38–44.

Cormack, Mike. *Ideology and Cinematography in Hollywood, 1930–39.* New York: St. Martin's Press, 1994.

Cowie, Peter. *Coppola: A Biography,* rev. ed. New York: Da Capo, 1994.

Critten, David, ed. *Film Guide,* rev. ed. New York: HarperCollins, 2008.

Dick, Bernard F., ed. *Columbia Pictures: Portrait of a Studio.* Lexington: University Press of Kentucky, 1992.

Doherty, Thomas. *Hollywood's Censor: Joseph Breen.* New York: Columbia University Press, 2007.

Dudek, Duwane. "Penn Crackles in Violent *Gangster.*" *Milwaukee Journal Sentinel,* January 11, 2013, sec. E: 3.

Ebert, Roger. *Movie Home Companion*. New York: Andrews, McMeel, and Parker, 2000.

Eisner, Lotte. *Fritz Lang*. Gertrude Monder, trans. New York: Oxford University Press, 1977.

Elert, Nicolet, Andrew Sarris, and Grace Jeromski, eds. *International Dictionary of Films and Filmmakers*, rev. ed. 4 vols. New York: St. James Press, 2000.

Estrin, Mark W., ed. *Orson Welles: Interviews*. Jackson: University Press of Mississippi, 2002.

Faulkner, William. *Sanctuary*. New York: Vintage Books, 1991.

Gifford, Barry. *The Devil Thumbs a Ride and Other Unforgettable Films*. New York: Grove Press, 1988.

Goodwin, Michael, and Naomi Wise. *On the Edge: The Life and Times of Francis Coppola*. New York: Morrow, 1989.

Grant, Barry, ed. *Fritz Lang: Interviews*. Jackson: University of Mississippi Press, 2003.

Greene, Graham. *The Graham Greene Film Reader: Reviews, Essays, Interviews, and Film Stories*, David Parkinson, ed. New York: Applause Books, 1994.

———. *A Gun for Sale*. New York: Penguin, 2005.

Griffith, Richard, and Arthur Mayer. *The Movies*, rev. ed. New York: Simon & Schuster, 1970.

Grobel, Lawrence. *The Hustons*. New York: Scribner's, 1989.

Gunning, Tom. *The Films of Fritz Lang: Allegories of Vision and Modernity*. London: British Film Institute, 2000.

Hamblin, Robert W., and Charles A. Peek, eds. *A William Faulkner Encyclopedia*. Westport, Conn.: Greenwood Press, 1999.

Hammen, Scott. *John Huston*. Boston: Twayne, 1985.

Hannsberry, Karen Burroughs. *Bad Boys: The Actors of Film Noir*. Jefferson, N.C.: McFarland, 2003.

Hanson, Curtis Lee. "William Wellman: A Memorable Visit with an Elder Statesman." *Cinema* 3 (July 1966): 22.

Hecht, Ben. "The Front Page: Now and Then." November 18, 1961, Ben Hecht Papers, Newberry Library, Chicago.

Herman, Jan. *A Talent for Trouble: The Life of Hollywood's Most Acclaimed Director, William Wyler*. New York: G. P. Putnam's Sons, 1995.

Heylin, Clinton. *Despite the System: Orson Welles versus the Hollywood Studios*. Chicago: Chicago Review Press, 2005.

Higham, Charles. *The Films of Orson Welles*. Los Angeles: University of California Press, 1973.

Higham, Charles, and Joel Greenberg. *The Celluloid Muse: Hollywood Directors Speak*. New York: New American Library, 1972.

Hoagwood, Terrence. "William Wyler's *Dead End*." *Literature/Film Quarterly* 41, no. 1 (Winter 2013): 19–28.

Horne, Philip. "Polanski and the Grotesque." *Sight and Sound* 23, no. 2 (February 2013): 40–43.

Huston, John. *An Open Book*. New York: Knopf, 1980.

Jameson, Richard. "John Huston." *Film Comment* 16, no. 3 (May–June 1980): 25–56.

Johnson, Robert. *Francis Ford Coppola*. Boston: Twayne, 1977.

Jones, Jenny, ed. *The Annotated Godfather*. New York: Black Dog and Leventhall, 2007.

Kael, Pauline. *For Keeps: 30 Years at the Movies*. New York: Penguin, 1996.

———. *Kiss Kiss Bang Bang*. New York: Bantam, 1969.

———. *Reeling*. New York: Little, Brown, 1976.

———. "*You Only Live Once*." *New Yorker*, July 24, 1995, 25.

Kaplan, Ann. *Fritz Lang: A Guide to References and Resources*. Boston: G. K. Hall, 1981.

Katz, Ephraim, ed., with Peter Nolen. *Film Encyclopedia*, rev. ed. New York: HarperCollins, 2008.

Kaufman, Stanley, and Bruce Henstell, eds. *American Film Criticism*. New York: Liveright, 1972.

Kehr, Dave. "Dark Crimes." *New York Times*, December 9, 2012, sec. 2: 19.

———. "A New Stream for the Thirsty." *New York Times*, May 26, 2013, sec. 2: 9, 13.

———. "Setting the Ground Rules for Noir." *New York Times*, December 7, 2012, sec. 2: 19, 23.

———. "Thrills from British Vaults: *No Orchids for Miss Blandish*." *New York Times*, June 18, 2010, sec. 2: 13, 18.

———. "Von Sternberg: Chief Director of Private Dream Factory." *New York Times*, August 20, 2010, sec. 2: 10, 22.

Kemp, Philip. "The Five Key Fitzgerald Films." *Sight and Sound* 23, no. 6 (June 2013): 5–19.

Keyser, Les. *Martin Scorsese*. Boston: Twayne, 1992.

Keyser, Les, and Barbara Keyser. *Hollywood and the Catholic Church: The Image of Roman Catholicism in American Movies*. Chicago: Loyola University Press, 1984. Includes films that deal with the Italian and Irish mafias.

Klein, Andy. "Fritz Lang." *American Film* 14, no. 12 (October 1990): 58.

Kobler, John. *Capone*. New York: Da Capo, 1971.

Koszarski, Richard, ed. *Hollywood Directors: 1941–71*. New York: Oxford University Press, 1971.

Koziol, Ronald, and Edward Baumann. "How Frank Nitti Met His Fate." *Chicago Tribune*, June 29, 1987, sec. 4: 1.

Kuehl, John, and Jackson Byer, eds. *Dear Scott/Dear Max: The Fitzgerald–Perkins Correspondence*. New York: Scribner's, 1971.

Laffel, Jeff. "Sylvia Sidney." *Films in Review* 45, nos. 9/10 (September–October 1994): 2–19.

Leblanc, Gerard, and Brigette Devismes. *Le Double Scenario chez Fritz Lang*. Paris: Armand Colin, 1999.

Lebo, Harlan. *The Godfather Legacy*. New York: Simon & Schuster, 1997.

Leitch, Thomas. *Crime Films*. 2002. Reprint, New York: Cambridge University Press, 2009.

Lim, Dennis. "It's All about a Dishonest Day's Work." *New York Times*, October 1, 2010, sec. 2: 1, 13.

Long, Robert Emmet, ed. *John Huston: Interviews*. Jackson: University Press of Mississippi, 2001.

Maltin, Leonard, ed. *Leonard Maltin's Classic Movie Guide*, 2nd ed. New York: Plume, 2010.

Marsden, Michael T., John Nachbar, and Sam L. Grogg, eds. *Movies as Artifacts: Cultural Criticism of Popular Film*. Chicago: Nelson-Hall, 1982.

Martin, Douglas. "Joseph Blotner, Faulkner Expert." *New York Times*, November 23, 2012, sec. B: 12.

Mason, Fran. *American Gangster Cinema: From* Little Caesar *to* Pulp Fiction. New York: Palgrave Macmillan, 2002.

Mast, Gerald, and Bruce Kawin. *A Short History of the Movies*, rev. ed. New York: Longman, 2008.

Mayfield, Sara. *Exiles from Paradise: F. Scott and Zelda Fitzgerald*. New York: Dell, 1974.

McArthur, Colin. *The Big Heat*. London: British Film Institute, 1992.

———. *Underworld USA*. New York: Viking, 1972.

McCarty, John. *The Films of John Huston*. Secaucus, N.J.: Citadel Press, 1987.

———. *Hollywood Gangland: The Movies' Love Affair with the Mob*. New York: St. Martin's Press, 1993.

McFarlane, Brian. *An Autobiography of British Cinema by the Actors and Filmmakers Who Made It*. London: Methuen/British Film Institute, 1997.

McGilligan, Patrick, ed. *Backstory: Interviews with Screenwriters of Hollywood's Golden Age*. 3 vols. Los Angeles: University of California Press, 1986–1997.

———. *Fritz Lang: The Nature of the Beast*. New York: St. Martin's Press, 1997.

McGivern, William. "Flashback: Roman Holiday." *American Film* 8, no. 12 (October 1983): 47–54.

McGrath, Charles. "Filmed to a Pulp." *New York Times*, June 6, 2010, sec. 2: 1.

———. "Fitzgerald as Screenwriter: No Hollywood Ending." *New York Times*, April 22, 2004, sec. A: 1, 23.

———. "An Orgiastic *Gatsby*? Of Course." *New York Times*, May 3, 2013, sec. 2: 2.

Miller, James. *F. Scott Fitzgerald: His Art and His Technique*. New York: New York University Press, 1967.

Munby, Jonathan. *Public Enemies, Public Heroes: Screening the Gangster from* Little Caesar *to* Touch of Evil. Chicago: University of Chicago Press, 1999.

Murray, Edward. *The Film Classics*. New York: Unger, 1978.

Nash, Jay Robert, and Stanley Ralph Ross, eds. *Motion Picture Guide, 1927–83*. 12 vols. Chicago: Cinebooks, 1985.

Neibaur, James. *Tough Guys: The American Movie Macho*. Jefferson, N.C.: McFarland, 1989.

Nobel, P., ed. *British Film Yearbook, 1949–50*. London: Skelton Robinson, 1949.

Nolan, Jack Edmund. "Graham Greene's Films." *Literature/Film Quarterly* 2, no. 4 (Fall 1974): 302–9.

Nugent, Elliott. *Events Leading Up to the Comedy: An Autobiography*. New York: Trident Press, 1965.

Oliver, Kelly. *Noir Anxiety*. Minneapolis: University of Minnesota Press, 2003.

Orwell, George. *Decline of the English Murder and Other Essays*. Harmondsworth, UK: Penguin, 1965.

Osteen, Mark. *Nightmare Alley: Film Noir and the American Dream*. Baltimore, Md.: Johns Hopkins University Press, 2013.

Ott, Frederick. *The Films of Fritz Lang*. Secaucus, N.J.: Citadel Press, 1979.

Parrish, James, and Michael Pitts. *The Great Gangster Pictures*. Metuchen, N.J.: Scarecrow, 1976.

Phillips, Gene, and Rodney Hill, eds. *Francis Ford Coppola: Interviews*. Jackson: University Press of Mississippi, 2004.

Phillips, Michael. "Audiences Love a Bad Guy." *Chicago Tribune*, January 11, 2013, sec. 4: 6.

Pinkerton, Nick. "Lang the Defiant." *Sight and Sound* 23, no. 1 (January 2013): 112–13.

Polito, Robert, ed. *Farber on Film: Film Writings of Manny Farber*. New York: Library of America, 2009.

Poniewozik, James. "The Original Jersey Shore." *Time*, September 27, 2010, 63.

Pye, Michael, and Linda Myers. *The Movie Brats: How the Film Generation Took Over Hollywood*. New York: Holt, Rinehart, and Winston, 1979.

Rizzik, Melena. "Awkward Bedfellows." *New York Times*, February 14, 2013, sec. 6: 1.

Robertson, J. C. *The Hidden Cinema: British Film Censorship in Action.* London: Routledge, 1989.

Rolfe, Hilda. "The Perfectionist." *Film Comment* 28, no. 6 (November–December 1992): 2–4.

Rollyson, Carl. *Lillian Hellman: Her Legend and Her Legacy.* New York: St. Martin's Press, 1988.

Russo, Vito. *The Celluloid Closet: Homosexuality in the Movies.* New York: Harper & Row, 1987.

Schillaci, Anthony. "*Bonnie and Clyde:* A Catholic Comment." *Film Comment* 4, no. 3 (Summer 1968): 49.

Schotter, Jesse. "Welles, Conrad, and Narrative Form." *Literature/Film Quarterly* 41, no. 1 (Winter 2013): 39–51.

Scott, A. O. "Big Bang Theories: Violence on Screen." *New York Times*, February 28, 2013, sec. 2: 13.

———. "Finding Drama in New-Fangled Filmmaking." *New York Times*, August 31, 2012, sec. C: 1.

———. "Seen This Guy Lately? Al Pacino." *New York Times*, April 2, 2003, sec. 2: 11.

Server, Lee. "The Last Gangster: Marc Lawrence." *Film Comment* 33, no. 3 (May–June 1997): 60–67.

Shadoian, Jack. *Dreams and Dead Ends: The American Gangster Film*, 2nd ed. New York: Oxford University Press, 2003.

Shapiro, Laura, and Ray Sawhill. "The First Untouchable." *Newsweek*, June 22, 1987, 68.

Stables, Kate. "*Gangster Squad.*" *Sight and Sound* 23, no. 3 (March 2013): 96.

———. "*You Only Live Once.*" *Sight and Sound* 22, no. 7 (July 2012): 121.

Telotte, J. P. *Voices in the Dark: The Narrative Patterns of Film Noir.* Champaign: University of Illinois Press, 1989.

Thew, Harvey. *The Public Enemy: A Screenplay.* Henry Cohen, ed. Madison: University of Wisconsin Press, 1981.

Thomson, David. *New Biographical Dictionary of Film*, rev. ed. New York: Knopf, 2010.

———. *Rosebud: The Story of Orson Welles.* New York: Vintage Books, 1997.

Vallon, Guilia D'Agnola. "Last Neo-Traditionalist Standing." *Film Comment* 49, no. 1 (January–February 2013): 54–58.

Warshow, Robert. *The Immediate Experience: Movies, Comics, Theater, and Other Aspects of Popular Culture.* Cambridge, Mass.: Harvard University Press, 2001.

Welles, Orson, and Peter Bogdanovich. *This Is Orson Welles*, rev. ed. New York: Da Capo, 1998.

Welsh, James M., and John Tibbetts, eds. *Encyclopedia of Filmmakers*. 2 vols. New York: Facts on File, 2002.

———. *Encyclopedia of Novels into Film*. New York: Facts on File, 2005.

———. *Encyclopedia of Stage Plays into Film*. New York: Facts on File, 2001.

Welsh, James M., and Thomas Erskine, eds. *Video Versions: Film Adaptations of Plays on Video*. Westport, Conn.: Greenwood Press, 2000.

Welsh, James M., Gene Phillips, and Rodney Hill, eds. *The Francis Ford Coppola Encyclopedia*. Lanham, Md.: Scarecrow, 2010.

Wexman, Virginia Wright. *A History of Film*, 7th ed. New York: Allyn & Bacon, 2010.

Yaquinto, Marilyn. *Pump 'Em Full of Lead: A Look at Gangsters on Film*. New York: Twayne, 1998.

INDEX

INDEX

ABOUT THE AUTHOR

Gene D. Phillips, S.J., is author of several works on film and literature, including *Beyond the Epic: The Life and Films of David Lean* (2006), *Some Like It Wilder: The Life and Controversial Films of Billy Wilder* (2010), and *Out of the Shadows: Expanding the Canon of Classic Film Noir* (Scarecrow, 2011). He is also coauthor of *The Francis Ford Coppola Encyclopedia* (Scarecrow, 2010).